There Ain't No Such Animal

There Ain't No Such Animal
and Other East Texas Tales

By BILL BRETT

Illustrations by

HARVEY L. JOHNSON

Texas A&M University Press

COLLEGE STATION AND LONDON

Copyright © 1979 by Bill Brett
All rights reserved

Library of Congress Cataloging in Publication Data

Brett, Bill, 1922–
    There ain't no such animal and other East Texas tales.

    1. Tales, American—Texas. 2. Folk-lore—Texas.
3. Texas—Social life and customs. I. Title.
GR110.T5B73   390′.09764′2   78-21777
ISBN 0-89096-069-2 (cloth)
ISBN 1-58544-073-6 (pbk.)

Manufactured in the United States of America
First Paperback Edition

To my wife, Anna Lou Palmer Brett,
and my sons, Terry Le Normand and John Key Brett

Contents

There Ain't No Such Animal	3
Old Fightin' Murphy	33
Uncle Jubal's Story about Mr. Stone's Trial	39
A Ghost Story	45
Justice	51
The Big Fight at Old Man Kyser's	57
A Twenty-Four-Hour, Seven-Days-a-Week Preacher	63
Horse Trading	71
The Killings	77
Just Talking	87
Courting	91
Death	97
A Three-Year-Old Unmarked Boar	103
The Education of Robert	107

There Ain't No Such Animal

There Ain't No Such Animal

No, I never knowed a completely honest man. I've knowed men that thought they was honest, men that claimed they was honest, and men that tried to be honest, but one that was completely honest, no, there ain't no such animal. Lots of men won't steal or cheat or beat you in any way, shape, form, or fashion, but there ain't never been a mortal man that hasn't lied, given the right circumstances.

I'll tell you how I learnt this. There used to be a man lived here, Old Man John Abbott, he's dead now, who was the most honest man I've ever knowed. Mr. John was one of these painfully honest men. If you and him was on a horse trade, he'd spend two hours telling you all his faults and then wake you up next morning to tell you something he'd forgot and offer to trade back if you weren't satisfied. Or maybe you'd buy a little corn from him and ever' basket had to be filled up, shook down, and run over, and then he'd put a extra one on your wagon, and even after that, apt as not, he'd say something about it being pretty weevily and maybe he'd better come down on the price a little.

Now, you'd think a man like that would be took advantage of regular, but he wasn't. Some folks wouldn't, and public opinion kept others from beating him. The few that done it didn't have much standing in this country afterwards, and people was so few then that a man tried to keep the respect of his neighbors because he knowed sooner or later he'd need their help.

There Ain't No Such Animal

Yes, sir, John Abbott was knowed as a honest man. When a man said another'n was "nearly as honest as John Abbott," he was praising him about as high as he could. I had knowed him and had heard folks talk about him for years, but it never struck me that there'd bound to be a reason for his ways till once't me and him was hog hunting.

Nearly ever'body through this Big Thicket country had hogs in the woods them days. They was pretty nearly a necessity for meat and grease and soap and was something that could be tended to in the winter when a man wasn't tied up with his crop. I guess around here was as good a hog range as there was any place in the world, but over in the Trinity bottom was the best of it on account of the pecans and acorns. 'Course that was before the timber companies raped this country. Now a crow would have to carry rations to cross there. Well, anyway, over there is where most of our hogs was, and the week before this happened me and Papa and Mr. Abbott had camped over there four or five days at a hog camp folks had got together and built years before, and had pretty well marked and tended to all our pigs and shoats and had drove eighteen or twenty bar' hogs out to home to butcher.*

'Course we'd have to do more hog hunting before the winter was over, but we'd be a month or two butchering and putting up what we had. We didn't figure on doing any more before we was through with that. Three or four days after we'd got home Mr. Abbott come to the house one morning and ask' Papa if he could go back over there with him. Told us that Abner Leggett and his boys had been over there hog hunting and had found one of his sows with a pig following her with Mr. Abbott's mark on it.

Well, that happened pretty often, since it was open

---

* A "bar'" hog is a barrow, or a boar that has been castrated.

range and sometimes hogs would change to another bunch. What a feller would do when there was two or three ear-marks in a bunch he'd penned would be to watch awhile and see what pigs was following and sucking what sow, and put the sow's mark on the pig. When a man found a pig following one of his sows with another man's mark on it, he'd generally change it hisself or mention it to the man that done it, and the next time the feller penned that bunch he'd change it. That was the accepted way to do it and worked fine for ever'body. 'Cept John Abbott. Mr. Leggett hadn't changed the mark on that pig and had only mentioned it to Mr. Abbott so he'd know it and wasn't a bit worried about that pig, but John Abbott weren't about to leave his mark on another man's hog one minute more then he could help. Well, Papa had all that meat to tend to and keep a smoke under, and tried to talk him out of it, but directly he seen he couldn't, so he told me I'd have to go. Time I'd shelled enough corn to fill my saddle-wallet—that'd feed my horse and have a little over to rally hogs with—and saddled up, he'd sacked up what leftover bread and meat Mama had and ground me some coffee, and me and Mr. Abbott left out.

Well, sir, it was a clear, cold day and we rode pretty brisk and steady to stay warm. 'Long a good bit before dinnertime we got in the country where the particular hogs we was looking for ranged, so we hissed the dogs out and went to hunting. They found and bayed several bunches, but none of them was the hogs we was looking for, so we'd just throw them a little corn so's they'd rally good next time, and call the dogs off and keep hunting. We called the dogs behind and put out for camp in time to get there and drag up firewood before dark and make a bucket of coffee. We hadn't any dinner and that cornbread and cold meat and that lye coffee beat any steak I ever seen on a table.

We was both pretty tired after we'd stopped awhile. It'd rained a lot that winter and the bottom was awful boggy. Pulling through mud was always hell on men and horses, but I ain't never seen a man that didn't like to set 'round a campfire and drink coffee and talk and yarn, no matter how tired he was. That's what me and Mr. Abbott done, and of all the stories I ever heard, I guess the one he told me that night was the best. And the damndest thing I ever heard. I believed it then and I believe it now.

I don't know yet how come me to ask the question that started him off. We'd both just slacked off there, soaking up heat and getting a swallow of coffee now and then and talking about dogs we'd knowed and horses and hunts we'd been on and how clear the night was, you know that kinda talk, and directly I says, "Mr. John, how come you're so all-fired honest?"

Well, he never said nothing for maybe three or four minutes, just set looking way deep in the fire like maybe he was recollecting. I'd about decided I'd made him mad, when finally he says, "Jody," he says, "I'm going to tell you something I ain't never told nobody, they ain't a living soul but me ever knowed about it, but it may help you be honest without going through what I did."

"When I was about eighteen or nineteen I left home and went out in West Texas and stayed gone five or six years. When I finally got a bellyful of cowboyin' and driftin', I come back home ready to settle down. Ma and Pa had both died while I was gone and my brother had got the home place, which was right, since he'd stayed there and worked and helped while I was running wild. But anyway, I was welcome to stay there long as I wanted to. Well, I helped him get a crop in and figured on getting on with one or the other of the cowmen around there, but that was the year we had the first bad depression in this country, and there wasn't no work nor no money. 'Course, we had plenty to eat because we raised it. No work nor no money wouldn't have bothered me much, but I'd got to sparking a girl just down the road. I'd knowed her all her life, but she'd growed up after I left. I had already popped the question, and she'd allowed she was ready when I was. Well, sir, I was ready then, and Bubba said we could move in with him and his brood, but I thought more of that girl than a pack-mule does a bell-mare, and I was bound and determined I'd have a little land and a house when we was married.

Bubba had a little ten-acre piece of good ground about two or three miles from him over to the east he said I could have for ten dollars a acre. It was just what I wanted, and this would be my biggest outlay, but even with lumber at eight dollars a thousand, I'd need another seventy or eighty dollars to build a house—figuring doors, nails, and windows —and some kind of a barn and chicken house. Well, sir, I thought and figured and cut here and trimmed there, but it looked like about two hundred dollars was what I'd have to have. Bubba said he'd deed me the land and I could pay him when I got able, but I knowed I'd have enough on my mind without having a debt hanging over my head.

Well, I tried. I looked for work, I didn't ask about wages or how many hours but just ask' for a job. I went to sawmills and ranches and farms. I even went to Beaumont hoping to find something, but the sawmills were mostly laying off and shutting down, and cotton weren't worth planting, and when you could sell one, a cow brute didn't bring but ten or twelve dollars. There just weren't no work.

Well, like I said, I'd tried, but it was either move that girl into a one-room log house built out in the woods on mortgaged land or get the money some way besides working. What it come down to was steal it.

I guess maybe I'd been thinking it'd wind down to that, for I already had a plan in mind as to how to go about it. There was an old feller lived down close to the county seat, a ol' bachelor, that had cattle scattered for twenty miles or so up through the Trinity bottom. I decided my best bet was to drive a bunch of his dry cows plumb out of the country, sell 'em for what I could get, and explain the money some way.

Well, no sooner decided than I went to getting ready. It was along pretty late in September, and we'd already got Bubba's corn crop in the barn. I went to feeding my horse all the flat grain he'd eat without foundering hisself. Ever' night I'd steal a few leftovers from supper. I was getting ready and waiting for the right conditions. The mosquitoes and black gnats were so bad in the woods that I knowed there wouldn't be anybody hunting or fishing just then, but just to be sure I wasn't seen, I wanted a spell of bad weather to keep folks indoors. I guess I waited maybe two weeks before it blowed in a bad spell. It got a little worse than I really wanted before it was over, must have rained five or six inches in two days and nights, but the morning I left Bubba's—I told him I was going looking for work—it was just a good gentle rain falling. I'd got up earlier than usual that morning, before Bubba, and had fed everything and got my leftovers and a couple of feedings of corn sacked up and ready to go. I went back in the house before I saddled up and got another cup of coffee and told them bye and to look for me back when they seen me coming. When I went out the door I told Bubba I'd turn his horses out and shut his dogs up in the crib so's they wouldn't follow me and he could stay in out of the rain.

I was saddling up when a thought struck me about my horse. He was a good sound animal, good under a saddle doing anything you put him at, but he was a West Texas horse and hadn't never been in the mud much. The way it was raining, we was going to have plenty of that. The more I thought of it, the more certain I was that heavy mud would whip that dry-country horse before dark. I finally decided I'd better ride one of Bubba's. He had two he was feeding that he used for work and riding, a little blocky bay that'd work a mule down in the harness and a ol' tall, rawboney, roman-nosed brown. Jumped ever' time you got on him but tougher than a wood-hauler's behind. The bay was so slow under a saddle he could travel all day in the shade of the same tree. That ruled him out, so it'd have to be the brown. I knew the brown had been raised down on the salt grass and could take the mud. When I finally decided the brown was the horse, I went back and hollered at Bubba that I thought I'd overfed my horse and was it all right if I took ol' Sam. 'Take him,' he says, 'and don't worry about your saddle, he'll come home.' Meaning he figured he'd throw me down and get loose with my saddle.

I figured he knew his own horse, so I didn't take any chances. I saddled him and got on him in the pen and got a-holt on my saddle front and rear and hung the steel in him. Man, he did break in two, but I had the advantage if the saddle stayed, and I just kept spurring until he picked his head up and quit.

I turned the other two horses into the pasture and opened the crib door before I left. Leaving the door open was so Bubba would think his dogs had got out and was off tromping around somewhere. Thinking that, he wouldn't worry about them for a day or two.

I stayed on the road for maybe a half mile and then

turned off into the woods and headed for the river. It was raining harder, but I didn't worry about getting lost. The only talent I was born with was knowing where I was. It don't make any difference whether it's cloudy, night-time, or thick woods, I always know where north is. Hog sense, Papa called it.

I was maybe two hours making the five or six miles to the Trinity going through the woods like that and maybe another hour following up it before I found cattle. A nice bunch, thirty or thirty-five head. One bull, fourteen or fifteen cows with calves still on them, and the rest dry cows. Most of the cows with calves had brands I didn't know, but the dry cows and the bull carried the ol' bachelor's brand. Not having calves on them showed they'd already been worked that fall and wouldn't be missed for a while. That suited me fine.

I let the two dogs bay them awhile and then rode in and started them up the river. I just kinda hung off to the side, just close enough to keep them traveling, and ever' time a cow with a calf got a little behind the bunch, I'd ride in and cut her out and leave her. They was glad enough to get their calves away from them barking dogs and didn't try to follow.

I musta been five miles following up that river before I had the bunch shaped up like I wanted. Wound up with twenty-six cows, the bull, and four big calves. Soon as I dropped the last cow and small calf, I turned the others into the river, not plumb sure I could make 'em take the water, but it was low enough they didn't give me any trouble. Didn't come much higher than ol' Sam's belly.

They was driving good, but I knew soon as they noticed they was getting out of their usual range I'd have trouble. I got them, I guess, a mile from the river before they started trying to break back and would have if it hadn't been for the dogs. I was trying to head west, straight away from the river, but the best me and the dogs could do was keep them going pretty well north. Bubba's ol' Janie bitch had already had to latch onto a big old high-horned cow's nose to turn her back, and I'd about decided we was going to spill the whole bunch, when we hit a wide, boggy slough heading pretty well northwesterly. They still wanted to go home, but not bad enough to risk bogging down, and by not having to watch that side we could keep 'em bunched and traveling pretty good. I still don't know if we'd have held 'em if the rain hadn't shifted to the east and went to falling a flood. Cattle turn their rumps to something like that and drift, and all I had to do was stay with 'em. No trouble, just miserable as hell. We crossed several brakes that was getting pretty full of rain water, but they was low enough we didn't have to swim but maybe a few yards. Them ol' river-bottom cattle was used to that and took the water like ducks. I 'spect ever' slough and brake in that country was big swimming by dark, but we topped out into the piney woods a little after midday, I guess, and didn't have to worry about it.

We wasn't in pine country but maybe two miles and then come out on a big prairie. The rain had eased up some by then but hadn't quit by any means, and I went to driving hard to get as far as I could while my tracks was washing out behind me. And while it was raining hard enough to keep folks indoors.

West was still my direction, but about the middle of the evening I hit a wide dirt road running a little more north than west and decided to follow it. I was pretty sure it'd take me to a railroad up the country somewhere. Barring any mischance, I'd decided to load them cows out for the Fort

Worth stockyards consigned to a commission-house buyer I knew there. I wasn't sure if he'd buy 'em, but he'd at least pay the freight bill. All I could do was ship and hope.

I drove into timber about good dark and just stepped down and unsaddled and staked ol' Sam and set down against a tree for the night. The rain had slacked off to a slow drizzle, and I figured the cattle was tired enough they'd bed down in it and not drift. Even if they did, I couldn't stay with them through the woods.

It was a long night. A long, long miserable night, dozing off and waking up, dozing and waking, wet, cold, and miserable. I started once to get up and try to get my rigging on Sam and hit that road and find a house and a fire, but I got to thinking, no, if that old half-outlawed son of a bitch throwed me down and got loose here at night, I'd sure be in a fix, afoot with a bunch of stole cows. Tough it out, boy, I told myself, better here wet and cold then laying over there somewhere wet, cold, crippled, and afoot.

Time it got light enough to see, I was saddling up, and when I cheeked ol' Sam and stepped up on him, I didn't give a damn what he done; after that kind of a night I was spoiling for a fight. Guess he knew it, never even clamped his tail when I untracked him and rode out.

The cattle was up and starting to move out on their own, but they bunched up and hit the road again when the dogs got there. They was hungry and I'd have let them spread out and graze a little, but it was still raining hard enough to hide our tracks, and I figured I'd better keep moving. Cattle ain't much for feeding on wet grass anyway, so these wasn't too hard to move right along.

A while after daylight the rain slacked up and finally quit just before midday, and a little later we come out on a three- or four-hundred-acre prairie. Good grass, so I just quit driving and let the cattle go to grazing. Wet or not, they was ready for a bellyful of it.

I was setting there on ol' Sam letting him feed a little while I soaked up sunshine and fought the drowsies—you know how good a feeling that is—and just got rode right up on. I didn't know there was another human in ten miles until Sam picked his head up and looked off to the right and kinda blowed. I knew there was a rider there before I looked. Wasn't a hundred foot away and coming right on. I don't know what I could have done if I'd seen him sooner, but at least it wouldn't have scared me as bad.

'Howdy,' he says when he rode up, 'pretty nice little shower, wasn't it?'

Well, that eased my mind some. A man can't be on too serious a business when he makes a remark like that about a six-inch rain. 'Yes, sir, it was,' I told him, 'a good dust-settler.'

'I got a tomato can and some coffee,' he says. 'If you think them cows will be all right, let's ride over to the edge of the woods and find a pine knot and brew up a can.'

Bad as I wanted coffee, I didn't especially give a damn whether them cows was all right or not. If he wasn't a lawman looking for me, he was going to make a friend for life with that tomato can.

You could just step down anywhere in that country and pick up a rich lighter knot, and it didn't take him but a minute to find one and whittle off enough shavings to get a fire started. I took the can and dipped up some reasonably clean water out of a low place whilst he was doing that, and in about fifteen minutes we was drinking hot coffee out of that can, turn and turn about.

I could tell he was sizing me up, and I was eyeballing

him close as he was me. His clothes was rough as mine, but better goods, and he had a good saddle on a fine sorrel, a road horse judging from the easy running walk he'd showed. I couldn't tell why, exactly, but I knew he wasn't a native of these piney woods.

Directly he says, 'Good bunch of cows you got there. Just buy them?'

'No, raised them. It's too wet to do anything else, and I just rode out to see how they was doing.' Him not being a native, I thought I'd leave the impression I was, and maybe he'd ride on and forget he'd seen me.

He didn't buy it. I knew it when he stood up and unbuttoned his brush jumper so I could see he had a six-shooter stuck in his waistband. 'Look,' he says, 'I'm a cow buyer, and for twenty years I've been coming up through here between the Trinity and the San Jacinto two, three times a year. I don't know the brand on them cows, but I do know it ain't from this country. Besides, this piney-woods grass won't raise cattle big as them, them's river-bottom cattle. Now, I'm going to do some guessing. I guess you brought them cattle from east of the Trinity, and I guess you stole them cattle.'

I never felt more afoot in my life than I did when he come out with that. I thought, just my luck to run into probably the only son of a bitch in the country that can add two and two, and me with my big mouth had to furnish him the two and two. And no chance to jump him, him with that six-shooter. Don't go to dodging and fighting your head, boy, I told myself, forget about jumping him and try to talk your way out of this.

'Look,' I told him, 'you got no right coming around here calling me a cow thief—'

'No, you look,' he says. 'I may be wrong, and if I am,

I'll apologize, but all you've got to do to prove it is us ride over and show me your place. Mount up and lead out.'

So much for talking my way out. He had me, I knew it and he knew it. He'd been more or less fishing before, but when I just set there and didn't offer to get on my horse, he was certain.

'Don't look so sick,' he told me, grinning big, 'maybe it takes one to know one. Look, now, I said I'm a cow buyer, not a lawman. I get an order for so many head of a certain grade from a commission house, buy 'em cheap as I can, and make a dollar a head for my trouble. Been doing it for years, and my pa before me. I buy cattle from anybody, long as I get a signed bill of sale with two witnesses to it. Let's make another can of coffee and see if we can make a trade.'

It didn't take long to strike a bargain. He had me over a barrel and knew it and more or less just told me what I'd get. I guess he was fairer than he had to be, though. What it worked out to was I agreed to give him a bill of sale for the thirty-one head and help drive them to the shipping pens. For his part, he was supposed to pay me seven dollars apiece for twenty-six cows and the bull. The calves went with the cows and wasn't counted.

He'd make maybe five dollars a head off the bunch with absolutely no risk, since he'd have a bill of sale, and if anything come up, I'd be the one to go to the pen. Still and all, I figured, I'd have close to that two hundred dollars I needed. I had knowed it was going to be risky when I got into the thieving business. I could've just rode off, and there wasn't no way I could have been connected to them cattle, but I wanted that money. I suspect the reason he gave me as much as he did was because he thought I might just go on and leave. Then he'd either have had to leave 'em too, or else take 'em and stick his own neck out. That bill of sale with my name on it was really what he got for his 189 dollars.

He pulled another surprise on me when I asked him where he was going to get two witnesses.

'They'll be here after a while,' he says. 'I've got two men coming behind me with what cattle I've bought since I left Goose Creek. I rode on ahead to clear the cattle off this prairie so's we could hold ours here for a day or two while I made a circle and tried to buy a few more head. That won't be necessary now, though. With your bunch, I won't need any more, and we'll head out for New Waverly in the morning and ship from there.'

The two cowhands showed up with his cattle, maybe thirty head, about the middle of the afternoon, and we let the two bunches mix and graze until sundown. They'd sucked up plenty of water out of puddles and was well fed by the time we bedded them down about good dark. I didn't figure they'd move before daylight, but he had us night-herd anyway. The four of us took two-hour shifts, so I got plenty of sleep.

They carried a camp outfit and their grub and bedrolls packed on a little brown mule, so we had a hot supper and breakfast. The next morning they just repacked ever'thing on the little feller and turned him loose. I missed him two or three times that day, but when we found good grass about the middle of the afternoon and let the cattle spread out and go to grazing, he showed up.

The buyer told me the mule was about twenty-five and had been foaled by a saddle mare his daddy rode on his buying trips. He hadn't never done nothing besides follow a bunch of cattle since he was a colt. Said he'd rather have that little brown mule than another hand.

There Ain't No Such Animal

The buyer rode out for New Waverly when we broke camp the third morning, and left me and the other two to bring the cattle. One of them had been with him on two or three drives before and knew where to hold up and wait for him to get back.

He met us a little after midday, though, and told us to loose-herd the cattle and let them graze and move along easy, that we only had about four miles to go, and he wanted them full when we put them in the railroad shipping pens. He'd made arrangements to have three cattle cars spotted at the loading chutes that night, and we'd load out in time for a Fort Worth–bound freight to pick them up about seven the next morning.

We penned the cattle in time to separate them into equal bunches in three loading pens and tend to our horses and the mule in one of the holding pens before dark. The buyer told us, rather than cook, we'd walk uptown and he'd buy our supper, but I told them to go ahead and bring me some meat and bread when they come back. I was a good piece from home and didn't think there'd be anybody that'd know me, but the fewer people that seen me on that trip, the better I'd like it. Besides, I had some studying to do.

What I had on my mind was how to get the cash money out of them cattle. The buyer had made damn sure that first night he'd got me to sign the bill of sale, and I'd made damn sure I got a bank draft from him. Now that draft was good as gold, but it was on a Fort Worth bank. I'd either have to deposit it at a bank and let them get my money for me, and that'd take several days, or I'd have to take it to that Fort Worth bank and cash it. I couldn't see no way without going to Fort Worth, and I didn't have a dime to buy a ticket or eat on.

The buyer and his two hands come on back in a little

while and brought me a bite to eat, and we all bedded down soon after. I still didn't see no way of getting to Fort Worth and back.

The switch engine spotting the cattle cars woke us up around four the next morning. All of us finally managed to find enough splinters and chips and pieces of boards in the dark to boil coffee with and was squatted around cooling and drinking it when the buyer grumbled something about he hoped to hell the railroad didn't let none of this bunch get down and pile up like they did the last time he'd shipped.

'Look here,' I says, 'I ain't going to do nothing but ride out this morning. If you're worried about them cows, you buy me a ticket back to here and I'll ride the caboose on that freight to Fort Worth and watch they don't pile up on the way.' If he took me up, it'd sure help solve things for me. I'd still have to manage for something to eat, I'd be two days there and back and a two-day ride home, but I'd eat if I had to steal it.

He was a pretty danged fair man for a cow buyer. 'I'll do better than that,' he told me. 'I'll buy you a ticket and pay a dollar a day for two days if you'll do that. The company'll be glad to get out that light.' I've noticed it's easier to be fair on the other man's money. But whoever it was, he'd spend it if it was justified. He even paid the station agent fifty cents to feed and water my horse and look after my dogs while I was gone.

He wasn't putting out no charity, though. I earned what I got. The two or three times we stopped between there and the stockyards I walked to the cars on the ground, but the rest of the trip ever' hour or so I'd walk on top to the cars and lay down flat and hang my head over far enough to see the cattle was all right. Pretty risky at times.

Cattle was big enough business to the railroad back then that they didn't delay with them if they could help it, and they had us at the stockyards and unloaded by ten or eleven the next morning.

Soon as they all hit the ground, I caught a ride on a wagon to town and went to the bank with my draft. I'd had the buyer make it out to "Bearer" and was worried maybe I'd have trouble cashing it, but they just paid me off. I guess I wasn't the first dirty horse-smelling cowhand they'd cashed one for. My next step was the post office. I bought 188 dollars' worth of money orders and had the clerk make them out to me and put on as buyer a name I'd thought up. The last thing was to buy a stamped envelope and get the clerk to address it to me at home and get it in the mail. By getting him to do all this for me, I made sure nobody'd recognize my handwriting when the letter got to Bubba's.

Soon as that was done I was through at Fort Worth, and I headed for the depot to find out when the next passenger train was for New Waverly. The ticket agent said I had about an hour to wait and would have time to stop into the Harvey House and eat if I was hungry. I was hungry all right, but not at them prices. A man could eat up seventy-five or eighty cents in there before he knew it. I walked down the street to a grocery store and got just as full on cheese, crackers, sardines, and two big red apples for half as much.

I was maybe half as long getting back on the passenger as it'd took the freight coming up. I got off at the shipping pens about midnight and didn't find nobody but ol' Sam and the dogs. The cow buyer had already headed back to Goose Creek, I guess, buying on the way. Years later at a cattleman's convention in Houston was the only time after that I ever saw him. It was in a hotel lobby, and I wasn't plumb sure it was him until he caught my eye and unbuttoned his coat and throwed it back like he'd done the time he'd showed me the six-shooter. We just nodded to each other and passed on.

I slept in the depot waiting room that night and drank coffee and bought something I could eat in the saddle before I left for home the next morning. Ol' Sam acted plumb nice when I climbed on him and rode out, but I knew better than that. Sure enough, about a mile from town he damn near throwed me down with me watching for it. I didn't try to spur him like I'd done in the pen at home, just got hold of ever'thing I could and rode out the storm. He was a danged ol' fool, but I got to give him credit for one thing, he was a road horse. At sundown we was fifty miles toward home and I was carrying a sore-footed dog, but he was still going strong.

Just before good dark I seen a little dim light back off the road maybe two hundred yards, and it struck me there wasn't any reason why I couldn't spend the night with somebody if they'd take me in. I was far enough from them cows that I needn't worry about being seen. I turned my horse and rode through the woods, not bothering to look for no road, and come up on a big old run-down cabin with a fireplace at both ends. Before I was halfway to it, two or three dogs had started barking and I knew I'd be expected.

I hollered hello to the cabin anyway, just to be mannerly, when I stopped at the front gate. I waited a little bit and didn't get an answer and was fixing to holler again when somebody just down the fence says, 'Who is it?'

'A stranger,' I answered. 'I thought maybe I could spend the night and get a feed for my horse. I got a little money.'

'I don't take in nobody,' the voice told me. 'What you got up there in front of you?'

'I got a sore-footed dog. She wore off the bottom of her feet on this sand road and I had to pick her up a few miles back.' And damn tired of her I was, too, her smelling that much like a dog.

'Must have come a good piece to've done that.' He stood up from where he was squatted just inside the fence and come through the gate and finished. 'Well, get down, get down and come in. I can't turn away a crippled animal. Hand her here and take your horse around back. There's a trough by the back door you can feed him in. Just throw your rigging in the house. Corn's just inside the door.'

Time I got unsaddled and fed, he'd doctored my bitch's feet with bacon grease—that's the standard remedy, takes the soreness right out—and was putting what grub he had on the table. It wasn't much, a couple pieces of cornbread and some mustard greens and coffee, but I had enough 'hungry sauce' to go on it to sure make it good. 'Long about my second helping, he says, 'Stranger, are you partial to breakfast? Because if you are, you'd better save some of that potlicker. There ain't nothing else.'

I quit eating right then and went to telling him I was sorry but I didn't know that's all he had.

'Don't worry about it,' he says. 'I wouldn't have mentioned it, but I didn't want you to go without breakfast. I ain't been to town in a month or two and the skeeters are too bad to go a-hunting or I'd had more. I don't have much company and ain't prepared for it.'

I'd of bet he didn't have much company. He had ever'-thing he owned in that one big room, several sacks of corn against the back wall—I could hear two or three families of mice rustling in the shucks—all three of his dogs, tools, some homemade furniture and, so they'd be handy to the dogs, all his cooking pots setting on the hearth. I paid for my meal and bed that night by listening. Out there by the fence he'd sounded like he didn't like folks, but the truth was he was lonesome. I fell out of my chair two or three times before he noticed it and told me which bunk to take. There was a pair of greasy blankets on it and a old moss mattress that had more bumps than the Trinity does bends, but I died when I got to it. It was a damn sight more comfortable than a saddle with a dog in your arms. I guess the old feller was pretty typical of the people in this country back then. They didn't have much to offer when you stopped in, but you could bet on one thing, you was going to feel welcome.

I was on the road by sunup the next morning in good traveling shape, three or four cups of lye coffee in my belly, a dozen ears of corn in ol' Sam's, and the dog's feet doctored again. I stayed drawed up in a knot the first hour, waiting for that damn ol' horse to try to throw me down, but I finally decided he knew he was on the way home and didn't have nothing but that on his mind. I got a bite to eat at a crossroads store about noon and kept riding, feeling the same thing he did. We crossed the river, on a bridge this time, some before sundown and turned back north, eight miles from home. We'd made I guess forty miles, and I was hoping Sam had the last eight left in him, but he perked up when we made that turn and I quit worrying. He'd make it. The dogs didn't, though. I missed them four or five miles out, but I knew they'd come on in when they got rested, and kept riding.

I sure was a proud little feller when I turned off the road into Bubba's. I was tired, but I knew I'd of been a lot tireder if Sam hadn't been the road horse he was. I thought back over the trip we'd made and about halfway to the barn I says, 'Sam, even if you did try to get me two or three times, you're a damn good horse,' and kinda leaned forward and patted him on the neck, and the old cranky bastard broke in two and threw me—no, he more slung me—about fifteen feet and went on to the barn by hisself. Just wanted to show me he could, I guess. I worked him after that some, but I never give him another chance at me by getting on him. I did give him a cussing, though, while I was unsaddling and feeding him.

Bubba got me up the next morning wanting to know if I'd seen his dogs. 'Why, no,' I told him, 'they gone?' 'Been gone ever since the day you left. When I went to feed that evening the crib door was open and they been gone ever since.' I knew he was worried about them, they was good dogs, and I wanted to tell him they'd be in soon, but I never let on. I rode over to see my girl awhile after dinner, and when I got back they was home and I could tell he'd doctored their feet. If he suspicioned I'd lied, he never let on.

The mail rider brought my money the next day and the worst time of my life started. The ol' man I'd stole the cows from, let's call him Smith, was there when I got it and it seemed like for months it was the same way, ever' time I looked around, he was there.

We was on the front porch drinking coffee that evening, and the ol' man come down the road and got down and come in when Bubba hollered at him. It wasn't but a few minutes later the mail rider rode up and brought the letter in. I had to put on an act about being surprised, and yes, I knew the name on the return address, me and him had had a bunch of horses in partners when I left West Texas, and wonder why he was writing me.

Bubba's wife was dancing around telling me to open it, open it, and when I did and pulled the money orders out and said how much they was, she had a fit and throwed her arms around me and says as how now I could build that house for Betty.

'Yes, ma'am,' I told her, 'I'm going to Butler's sawmill tomorrow and haul enough to start on it.'

That's when Mr. Smith went to deviling me and never quit till he died. 'Tell you what, John,' he told me, 'I've got to take a load of stove wood to town to my sister's this week, and I'll just do it tomorrow and come by Butler's on the way back and haul a load for you.'

Well, I didn't want him to do it and told him not to bother, that I'd just go get it as I needed it, but he just insisted and I finally had to give in. That's the way he done me, helped a hundred times. While I was building he'd come by and stop and maybe work the rest of the day. When I was digging my well he happened by and seen how slow it was going—I'd go down and fill two buckets and then climb the ladder out and pull them up and empty them. It was slow all right, but he was there the next three days helping me.

Stayed with it until I got water sand and got the curb in. When I got married just before Christmas, he sent two goats and a good big shoat over to barbecue for the dance Bubba give. Not only that, we hadn't been married a week when he brought Betty a set of quilting frames for a wedding present.

And ever' time I seen him, I was reminded about ever'thing I had, even my wife, I had because I'd stole from him. I got to where I couldn't ever rest easy, it was always eating on me and ever' time he done me a kindness it got worse.

It finally got to the point to where I had to do something. I'd studied about it and twisted and turned looking for a way out, but all the time I knew there wasn't but one thing I could do to get it off my mind.

I saddled up one morning and rode out to go tell Mr. Smith I'd stole his cows.

If I'd been superstitious, if I'd took any stock in them old wives' signs about bad happenings, I'd of turned back before I'd went a mile. I'd had three of the worst ones you can get, according to an old aunt of mine, nearly before I was out of sight of the house. The first one was when I rode off. One of Bubba's dogs had took up at my house and always before when I left horseback or in the wagon he'd follow, but this time he just set at the front gate and howled. That was a little peculiar, but I'd heard dogs howl before with nothing bad happening and I didn't pay him no attention. I'd gone maybe a quarter-mile when I seen the second sign. I looked up ahead and just off the road in a patch of weeds I seen a big black snake's head sticking up. Aunt Addie had always told that the devil used snakes to carry messages, and when one took time on his errand to watch you, you was fixing to have bad trouble. After the howling dog—whether you actually believe in them or not, you notice signs—seeing the snake made me think on just how much trouble I might be letting myself in for. When you go confessing to a cowman you've stole some of his stock, you're asking for it, and them old-time cowmen would generally see you got it.

No matter, though. Whatever he done afterwards, I had to get it off my conscience. I guess I'd gone maybe another half-mile when I heard a kind of croaking up over my head, and when I looked it was a buzzard, sailing along nice and easy like they do. He made the same racket two or three times before he sailed on out of sight. I've heard them do that when they're feeding around a carcass, but that's the only time I ever heard one do it while he was flying.

Superstition or not, when that the third sign showed up, the surest one there is of trouble, I'd always heard, I got a few chills up my back and thought of maybe putting things off till tomorrow. I couldn't see doing that, though. It'd just mean another day and night of having it on my mind, and I had a feeling I should have already tended to it. It'd be a hard chore, but if I was ever going to have another day with an easy mind, I had to tell Mr. Smith.

I stayed on the road till it went into the open woods, and then I quit it and headed straight through to the old man's place. It was maybe three miles back there, and I guess I was over halfway there when I heard dogs barking. When I got up to where I could see, it was Mr. Smith with eight or ten cows and a big old line-backed steer. He was having lots of trouble trying to handle them.

Soon as he seen me, he pulled back and let the dogs have the cattle and waved me to come to him. When I rode up he says, 'Glad to see you, John. You got time to help me get this bunch to the house?'

'Be glad to, Mr. Smith,' I told him, 'but I got something to tell you first you ain't going to like.'

'I'll like it a damn sight less if that steer gets away,' he says. 'He's been in ol' Saul's field two or three times and has jumped in his yard once and whipped his womenfolk back in the house. I've tried to pen him twice but had to let him go, he got to fighting so bad. Two of us can rope the son of a bitch and lead him in.'

Nothing to do but help him. We moved in and he hollered at the dogs to get back and give them a little room, and for about a mile the race was on. We couldn't go ahead and slow them down without busting up the bunch, so we just rode the sides close enough to do something when the chance come, if it ever did. I'd about got my pony's bottom before we hit the road that went by the old man's house and his pasture fence right alongside it. That give us enough advantage, him ahead and me holding them against the fence, to get down to a walk.

The cows was driving fine, but me and Mr. Smith could both tell that steer was fixing to leave. Directly, the old man eased back close enough to talk to me and says, 'John, he's going south in a minute in spite of us. Tell you what let's do, let's get our ropes down and catch him before he leaves. My old horse is big enough to stop him, so I'll catch him first and you tie on and keep him off me. Untie your rope and dally it so if we get in a storm you can get loose. I'd hate for that steer to get away dragging you and that broomtail.'

Well, he'd laid it out just right, that was the way to do it. The big bay he was riding was almost big as the steer and could hold him, but the pony I was on wouldn't weigh in four hundred pounds of that steer. I'd traded my West Texas horse for a span of little Spanish mules and had bought the one I was riding off the prairie for six dollars and broke him. He was making a good horse, for what there was of him, but, as I heard a feller say one time, you could stick your nose in his behind and look down both sides. With Mr. Smith ahead leading the steer, though, and us behind, we'd drag heavy enough to keep him off the old man.

Well, it worked perfect, up to a point. After he'd said do it, we wasn't but a second getting our ropes ready and running into the bunch. Mr. Smith made a pretty throw, just popped it over them wide horns on that ol' bully, set his ol' bay down and swapped ends with him, and before he got straightened up, I come by and piled my loop on top of his.

What happened next was my fault, and the only excuse I can give is I wasn't no dally hand. I'd always kept my rope tied to my foretree just like ever'body in this timber country does, and would have this time if the old man hadn't said not to, and not being used to dallying, I didn't get but one wrap on my pommel before we hit the end of that thirty foot rope.

I couldn't hold it with just one wrap. It went smoking from around my pommel and jerked my hand in under the wrap and took most of the meat off the end of my forefinger. And left that ol' steer loose at my end.

I was pulling my horse before I lost my rope and it didn't take but a second or two to slow him down and swing around, but even quick as that was, the steer was almost onto the old man. I decided afterwards that his horse must have been pulling backwards against the rope, and when the steer run at him and give him slack, that horse couldn't get his feet back under in time to get out of the way. He'd just got wheeled sideways when the steer hit him and one horn went in just ahead of his flank and gutted him, ripped a hole a cat could crawl through. I guess he must have been clear of the ground. It looked like the steer just turned him over so easy, just laid him over broadside and he rolled half up, all four feet straight up and the old man still in the saddle.

I never checked up, just come back, squalling loud as I could, trying to get the steer's attention off the horse and Mr. Smith and onto me. I got it all right. He was wheeling toward me before I got there, and when I went by he come in behind, close enough he was picking up my little horse's tail with them long horns ever' jump. It seemed like we went ten times as far as we did before that race ended. Mr. Smith's rope wasn't no longer than mine, though, and still tied to his saddle, and when the steer hit the end of it that stopped it. I heard him hit the ground and looked back and he was broadside, head folded back under and deader'n hell with a broke neck!

When I seen that I iron-handed my pony to a stop and jumped off and got back to the old man quick as I could. His horse had rolled off him and was starting to get up, and I got in between and crowded him away from the old man so's he wouldn't stomp on him. It wouldn't have made no difference if he had. He got four or five breaths after I knelt down by him and it was over, Mr. Smith was broke all to pieces and dead.

I couldn't believe it. I straightened up and looked at what had happened and couldn't believe all that had happened in the last minute and a half. The steer dead, Mr. Smith laying dead, and his good bay horse standing there with his guts hanging to the ground.

I knew I'd have to go get somebody to come help, but I couldn't leave the horse suffering like that. I could tell there wasn't no saving him, so I stripped the saddle off and led him a few steps further and come back and got Mr. Smith's pistol out of the saddle pocket. I pulled the bridle off and petted him on the neck a little and stepped back and shot him between the eye and the ear. It was a good deed, but it was rough to have to do it.

I know it ain't so, but I'd like to think they all three went to a place like the Indians believed in, and Mr. Smith and his ol' horse got another chance to tie onto ol' Lineback. With better help that time.

I knew when I rode away from there I had a load I'd carry the rest of my life, that I couldn't shift it over to Mr. Smith now and pay for it anyway. I've carried it, too. I've never been able to look at anything I've ever owned without knowing I stole from a good man to begin with.

The day I helped lower the old man in his grave I

vowed that as long as I lived nobody else would ever be stole from or lied to by me, and I've done my best for forty years to see that it's so."

I didn't have nothing to say when Mr. Abbott quit talking. I'd asked him why he was so honest and damned if he hadn't told me. Even if it didn't help me keep honest, it was a dang good yarn.

We found the hogs we was looking for in an hour after we left camp the next morning, and Mr. Abbott cut his mark off old Abner Leggett's pig and we pulled out for home. I had an idea, knowing the old man, that if we hadn't found it we'd have made a hungry camp that night and hunted another day.

I didn't see the old man again until the night, about two weeks later, he was put up to be a deacon in our church. He'd joined the church just two or three years before and had really took it to heart. Worked at being a good member and a practicing Christian, and being a deacon was something he wanted but didn't think he was good enough for, and he said as much when they told him he was being considered for it.

He'd been told about it before church started, and right after the singing and collecting was over old Preacher Garrett called him up to the pulpit and told the congregation about it.

"Face the congregation, Brother Abbott," he says. "Now, is there anyone in the sound of my voice that knows any reason why Brother Abbott shouldn't be a deacon of this church?" When nobody spoke up, he says, "Brother Abbott, we all know you, but nonetheless we've examined your qualifications closely. We find you well qualified in our sight. However, we can never know you as well as you know yourself, and I ask you now, is there anything on your conscience you haven't confessed before God and man in His temple and received forgiveness for?"

I thought for a second he was going to come through, but all them friends' and neighbors' and fellow church members' eyes was more than he could stand. John Abbott said, "No, none."

Like I said to start with, there ain't no such animal as a man that won't lie, given the right circumstances.

Old Fightin' Murphy

THE first time, I guess, I ever seen old Fightin' Murphy was at a dance he had at his house. We'd been moved out here to the edge of the Thicket about a year and knowed ever'body else but hadn't met him because he'd been took up by the law and sent to the pen for two years for making whiskey. One of the Henson boys come by and told us about the dance and also told us about the old man and why he was nicknamed "Fightin'." Said Mr. Murphy was a good man and a good neighbor and was well liked and respected in the community and outside of making whiskey was very law abiding. His worst fault was when he got a few drinks in him he just had to fight somebody. Bradford Henson said the old man had give out he was having the dance to celebrate getting home, but he suspected that weren't the whole reason. Said the old man didn't have nothing at home but womenfolks, and while he was gone they had so much to do in the field they didn't have time to keep the place up much. The yard fence had got bad and the hogs had been sleeping under the house, and he thought the dance was mostly to get some of the fleas toted off.

Me and my brother Wallace was 'long about eighteen or nineteen then and all for them dances and play parties, and we sure wasn't going to miss this'n even if it turned out we was the ones had to do the fighting. Back then when somebody give a dance they just seen Doc Million or some other fiddler and ask' him if he'd come and bring a guitar player, and then put out the word as to when it'd be, and ever'body that heard of it was invited. As it happened, Wallace and me was especially ready for a dance just at that time. We'd put in all summer helping Pa break horses for Mr. Middlebrook and two, three more cattlemen from down on the salt grass, and we'd done so good he'd decided, since we mostly had our full growth, to order us a blue serge suit apiece from Sears, Roebuck. Suit styles didn't change much then, and when a feller got old enough he wouldn't outgrow it, he'd buy a blue serge suit, court in it, marry in it, wear it when he had to, and it would just get slicker and shinier and harder till it was a relief to see the thing go when he was buried in it.

Anyway, we'd got several days' work apiece that summer substituting on the road gang for men that'd rather pay than work out their road tax, so when Pa ordered our suits we just sent with it and got us a boiled shirt apiece. Wallace ordered blue but I got me a pure white one, and we both got a celluloid collar and bow tie to go with it. 'Course we couldn't wear our old boots with all that new stuff, so we got Pa to let us have what money we was short against us selling some hogs the next winter, and we sent our foot measurements off to Stockman-Farmer at Denver for new boots.

Well, sir, it seemed like good things just kept on happening to us that year. Grampa and Grandma Hollister come down from Honey Island for a visit right after that and 'course they didn't get done drinking coffee before we'd told them all about what we was getting. Grampa studied awhile and then allowed he couldn't have no grandsons of his wearing all that finery and still be half naked, and he had Grandma dig around in her reticule till she come up with three ten-dollar gold pieces. He handed them to us and said we was to buy us a Stetson hat. I imagine if Pa had let us go right then we'd have killed our horses getting to Liberty, but he held us off till Saturday.

Well, sir, in about three or four weeks the mail rider had delivered all that stuff, and we'd went and got our hats and had ever'thing but the boots hanging on the wall in our room where we could admire them and was just waiting for the occasion to blossom out. If Pa hadn't kept us at it I guess we'd have both just quit working and spent the whole time with the garments.

About two weeks before Mr. Murphy give the dance we'd got one helluva big rain and a bridge got washed out over on Big Boggy marsh, and the precinct road foreman, Mr. Arthur Dark, had hired me and Wallace a couple of days to help build it back, and Wallace had got a bridge timber on his hand and broke two or three bones. Mr. Dark told him he'd better knock off and ride into Liberty to a doctor and get it splintered up, so we saddled his horse for him and he was gone three or four hours, and when he got back instead of splints the doctor had folded his hand up and put a plaster-of-paris cast on it. It was the first cast we'd ever seen, but we could tell it was a big improvement over splints if you could keep the ticks and redbugs out from under it.

Well, the day for the dance took its time, but it finally did show up and the first thing me and Wallace done after we fed that morning was draw us up some water in two of Mama's washtubs and set it where it'd be in the sun all day so's we wouldn't have to bathe in cold water that evening. That was the longest day I guess I ever spent, but finally it got by and we swallered our supper in chunks and got bathed and borrowed Pa's old straight razor and scraped our jowls and suited up, new from boots to hat.

Man, we did look just perfect, according to us, except for Wallace's old cast. After him working with it on for two weeks, it was so durn dirty and filthy the puppies wouldn't even have played with it. Mama solved that for us, though, by ripping some strips off of a old sheet and bandaging it up.

We'd saddled our horses before we dressed, and quick as that cast was hid we lit out. It weren't but about four miles to Murphy's and we'd got off about sundown, but dances started then quick as enough folks got there to help move the furniture out of the front room, and this one was already warming up when we arrive. We kinda hung back and watched through the door till the musicians took a break and eased outside to get a drink, and then made our entrance. Feller, I want you to know, we made a bigger impression than a three-legged man at a behind-kicking. I can't say any of the girls there actually gasped with admiration, but three or four sure looked like they wanted to. It was just plumb satisfying.

Quick as the music started in again, we got with 'em and it was nothing but romping and stomping till about eleven, when Mr. Murphy's whiskey decided he had to fight somebody. Before we even knowed the fit was on him, he'd stopped the musicians and clumb up on a chair, and quick as we all stopped and got quiet he says, "Folks, you know I can put up with most anything, but there is one thing I cannot abide, and that is a man a-flaunting a white shirt at me in my own house. Now, I don't want any bad feelings afterwards, but I am going to whip ever' man in this room a-wearing a white shirt."

This sounded to me like maybe he was overly ambitious, and I went to looking around to see how many the old man was going to have to fight and discovered that there weren't nobody met his specifications but me. Time I looked back towards him he'd un-clumb his chair and was making for me, and there didn't seem to be nothing to do but get ready to fight. Wallace had been dancing with one of the Simms girls and was standing just in front of me and a little to one side, and just as Mr. Murphy got even with him, he reached over with that bandaged cast and hung one up side his head. Well, sir, that three or four pounds of plaster just folded the old man up and rolled him like a shot cottontail, and he couldn't have centered the door to the kitchen any better with a surveyor showing the way. Me and Wallace both figured we'd have to fight our way out, but before anybody could make a move towards us, Mr. Murphy staggered back into the doorway and caught hold of the jamb and says, "Boys," he says, "Don't fight on my account, but boys, if you mus' fight, for godalmighty's sake, watch that man with the sore hand."

I 'spect a drunk fifty is about as bad a age as there is.

Uncle Jubal's Story about Mr. Stone's Trial

THIS one was told by Uncle Jubal Black one night whilst a bunch of us set around a fire listening to a pack of hounds working on a fox trail.

"Most of y'all either knowed or has heard of ol' man Robert Stone, him that lived north of the Sam Houston place, up there where the Big Thicket falls off into the Trinity bottom. 'Course living in that country, about half of his eating was game he took out of the woods or fish out of the river or them lakes in back of the Nixon Smith place. There weren't many people in this country in them days, and lots of game, so even after the legislater up to Austin went to passing game laws saying when you could or couldn't kill deer and turkey and bear, it never affected Mr. Stone's way of living any.

Directly, though, two or three years later, the state sent one of them young game wardens into the country and 'long about the middle of the summer he was tromping around up there, probably lost, and happened upon the old man's place and found his hounds dragging a fresh deer hide around. Well, his shirttail didn't touch his behind till he got back to Liberty and went to the county judge and put charges against Mr. Stone for hunting out of season. Judge John Wentworth was a hunting partner of the old man's and had been for forty-odd years, and he knowed there weren't a jury in the county could be got that would convict him, but he figured maybe if he let it go to trial, it might slow Mr. Stone down a little and save trouble later on. Finally he fixed a warrant up, hoping he was right, and give it to the young feller and told him to be dang sure and take it to the sheriff to serve. Sheriff Bud Parkinson didn't know what was going on and said he didn't have time to tend to serving it, so the boy, being young and eager, wanted to go do it hisself.

'Course Bud knowed old man Stone and told the boy not only just no, but hell no! he wasn't going up in them woods trying to serve that warrant, that he didn't want to have to go up there and tangle with Mr. Stone a-trying to find out what happened to no dang game warden. 'Course he knowed all the time all he had to do was let the old man know he'd like him to be at Liberty on such and such a day and he'd be there, come hell or the fish biting, but he thought maybe if he put the warden off a few days, it'd blow over. The boy kept after him, though, till finally Bud went over and talked to the judge and then went and looked up the mail rider, James Palmer.

James' mail route went within about three miles of the Stone place, and the sheriff ask' him to ride by and tell Mr. Stone to come to court the next Monday and to tell him why. Well, the old man was there bright and early, and so was ever'body else over age fifty that knowed about it, and it was way up in the middle of the morning before we all got through howdying and shaking hands and visiting and John Wentworth climbed up in his pulpit and set down and said since Mr. Stone didn't have a lawyer, he'd just let the prosecuting attorney select the jury.

Well, sir, that sounded bad for Mr. Stone, but the county attorney then was Bubba Sivils, old man Arn Sivils' middle boy, and the Stones and Sivils had come to this country together when the Trinity was just a creek, so the old man got a pretty fair shake. Bubba never picked a man under seventy-five years old to serve. We figured up later that between the six, them jurors had knowed Mr. Stone about three hundred years.

Well, Bubba ask' that warden a few questions, but the young feller had seen how Mr. Stone had been treated and it seemed like his heart wasn't in his answers, even though they was the truth. After he stepped down, Judge Wentworth ask' the old man if he wanted to say anything.

'Yessir, John, I do,' he says. 'I've hunted with you forty years, and thirty before that with your pa, and you know in all that time I ain't never killed nothing but buck deer, and now them fellers up in Austin say the only time I can kill one is in wintertime. Why, you and ever' man in this room knows a buck ain't fit to eat that time of year. They's ruttin' and runnin' and their ol' necks is all swole up and dreanin' bloody water and they smells and tastes like a billy goat. Then when they get over that, they's so pore their meat's plumb blue the rest of the winter. Now you take that same buck 'long in July or August or September, he's so fat and slick a feller purely loves to peel the hide off and can't wait to get that backstrap out and in a skillet, and then when you gets inside, there's his kidneys pretty near covered up with fat and durn near enough leaf-fat to fry the rest of him. Ever' dang one of you fellers knows that, 'cept maybe that young city feller there.

'Now, John, what I'm trying to tell you, and them six men you got working for you up there, is that a buck deer ain't fit to eat in the winter, and is in the summer, and it were a mistake for them legislaters to open the season when they can't be used, and John, I ought not be held liable for no politicians' mistake!'

Well, sir, the jury went out and come back in about ten minutes and told Judge John Wentworth that they had reached an agreement but no verdict. They'd all agreed that they had a reasonable suspicion that Mr. Stone was right, but they didn't think they could ever bring in a verdict."

Well, that ended that for then, but——

"Boys, I do believe them hounds is fixing to jump. I just heard Rawlinson's ol' squalling dog open and if he does it again we'll have a fox race on our hands shortly. Now you fellers that's always a-talking be quiet and listen. There he is, boys, listen, he sounds like he's in mortal pain, now, listen, boys, listen, which dog is that putting in with 'em? Sounds like one of Roy's young dogs. No, it ain't, it's yore ol' Spot, Fred, ain't it? That's him, that's the one it is, boys, hear that mouth, clear as a blowing horn. There's both of yore pups now, Roy, and listen, boys, listen at that, Broom's old dog has cut across on Mr. Fox and is a-carryin' him on! Hear them others—hush, they's comin' to him! There's one come in with him now I ain't heard before. Is that that Trumbull hound you got at Woodville, Billie? I figured so. Listen, boys, listen, now them others is catching up, there's George's old Red putting in, and another'n, and Fred's dog, and one of them pups and my old three-legged dog, and there's Roy's other pup and Rawlinson's old bell-mouthed bitch and the whole pack is looking at that fox the way they're running. Boys, I tell you, boys, you'll never hear sweeter music than that till Gabriel calls you forth!"

I wish that night had never ended.

A Ghost Story

SURE, I've heard lots of ghost stories. It's always pleasured old folks to scare hell out of young'uns with them tales. They mostly had lots of chain rattling and moans and grabbing of folks and hair turning white over night and the usual things. Not always, though. Grampa had one he told regular about a feller passing a graveyard—nowadays they're cemetaries—and this feller looked back and seen a ghost behind him. Well, sir, the spirit, as the preacher says, moved him, and he took out down the road like a cat shot in the behind with rock salt. Grampa'd always say he was running like a steel-dust colt. After a couple of miles he was blowing like he was girted too tight and had a shoelace dragging besides, so he risked a look over his shoulder and didn't see nothing, and pulled up and set down on a log. About the time he bent over to tie his shoelace, Mr. Ghost set down by him and says, "Well we had a pretty good race, didn't we?"

"Yes sir," the feller says, "But it weren't nothing to the one we're gonna have when I get this shoelace tied!" Us kids always giggled and laughed through this one because we knew what was coming and was relieved about it.

I 'spect, though, what you're wanting to know is did I ever see a ghost. No, I never seen one, but twice I've had things happen I couldn't explain and can't till yet. The first time I was just a big ol' knotheaded boy. I was riding for Mr. R. R. Buford, and at the time we was camped over in the river bottom working cattle. This particular day we'd worked north from the mouth of Green's Bayou and throwed our gather, about sixty or seventy head of dry cows, on some made ground* at the foot of Baldwin Bend. These was easy handling cattle once they was got in hand, and it weren't no trouble for one man to hold them in the Bend.

I'd been sent by Mr. Buford that morning to ride in between Timber Brake and Five Run and push everything out to the north and towards the river, but before I got there, just off from Billie Green Slough, I hit five head of high rolling heifers and made a hell of a round, whipping down the hind legs ever' jump and try to get ahead, till I finally crowded them against Timber and turned them back. I was riding a damn good horse, but the return trip was about like the outgoing and me and them hell-fired heifers had pretty well got ol' Snow Biscuit's bottom by the time we caught up with the bunch. No, I don't know how he got that name, but knowing cowhands, there ain't a damn bit of telling.

Well, anyway, Mr. Buford left me to herd, since I was about afoot, and took the crew on up the river to gather his Windy Bend cattle.

According to some of them cowboy songs, herding cattle was plumb delightful, but most working hands hated the job. Especially if it was cold or raining. Just setting and looking and trying to stay awake, after the cattle settled down. About the only good part of it was having a chance maybe to eat. No, we didn't carry any grub, and they dang sure didn't bring us any. Cowmen them days didn't believe in spoiling hands with too many luxuries. I've heard it told of Mr. Sam Partlow—he run 2,000, maybe 2,500, head down around Liberty—that he hired his day hands on at a dollar and dinner and along about twelve or one o'clock he'd say, "Boys, it's dinner time," and they'd climb down and go

---

* *made ground*—where a stream overflows and washes in silt and sand. In this case the Trinity River had cut a new channel and filled in the old.

to gathering whatever was eatable and handy. They told on some cowmen that they hired at a dollar a day and a Mexican dinner. When twelve o'clock come you got down off your horse, pulled your belt up a notch, and got back on your horse. If we was working close to camp or the home place, we got fed, but other times we kept pretty steady company with "Miss Meal." Back then if you couldn't forage like Hood's Brigade, you'd pretty nigh starve to death working cattle. There was usually something eatable in season, but unless you was holding cattle you seldom had time to gather it. Along early in the spring mayhaws and redhaws would get ripe and then the blackberries and huckleberries. By the time them was gone, mustang and muskeydime grapes would be ready. Next would be wild tomatoes and persimmons and pecans beginning to fall, and we'd get a frost on the coon grapes and rattan balls a little later and sweeten them. 'Course, if the truth were knowed, we stole a good many roas'n'ears and taters when they was handy. I have made out on acorns, but it took a lot of chewing and spitting before you downed 'em, or they'd give you a helluva bellyache.

Well, anyway, the cattle had kinda scattered out, some laying down and some just standing and chewing their cud, and me and old Snow Biscuit having it plumb peaceful, me cracking and eating pecans I'd stepped down and picked up, and him standing on three legs half asleep. Directly, though, he straightened up and raised his head and went to pointing his ears ahead, and I noticed the cattle getting up and walking. Now, boy, remember, this was about two or three in the evening on a clear day and on made ground clean as the palm of your hand. Time them cattle quit moving, they was standing in a circle about thirty-five or forty foot across and ever' damn cow was looking at something in that circle!

Head up and ears out! My horse was standing stiff under me, still pointing his ears and looking hard as they was, and not moving a muscle. That circle weren't more than thirty, maybe thirty-five yards in front of me and *there weren't nothing in that circle. Nothing.* I'll make a deathbed oath to that. If it'd happened in a second or two, I wouldn't be so sure, but this went on for two or three minutes, and hard as I tried, never did I see a thing in that circle. Directly, my horse kinda blowed and slacked off on three legs again, and about the same time the cattle went to moving, not scared, just getting comfortable again. I had ever' backhair standing up like bristles on a biting sow and was fixing to put the gut-hooks to ol' Snow Biscuit and leave there, hunting company in a hurry, when I recollected that when the cattle settled down I'd slacked my girt so's he'd be a little easier. By the time I tended to that, I remembered Pa mentioning to me that long as you had a horse and could set a saddle you didn't leave cattle for no reason. I knowed old man Buford would tell him first time he seen him. Pa was the kind of man that believed the best way to put anything in a boy's head was hammer it in his backside with whatever was handy, long as it weren't deadly. This all run through my head in about a second, but it sure made me see where my duty laid and I clumb back up on my saddle and went back to eating pecans. I was still scared as hell and I couldn't do anything about that, but I was also hungry as hell and had them pecans, so I just took first things first, as the old saying goes. A little before sundown I heard Mr. Buford 'way cross the bottom, blowing two shorts and a long on his horn, and I knowed he wanted me to come on to camp. I was past ready.

    I ain't ever told this to nobody before, but I have studied about it lots of times. I've never decided whether them animals could see something, or just knowed something was there. Maybe they can see things folks can't, but there's one thing I know for sure and certain, *I* couldn't see nothing in that circle.

No, I ain't goin' to tell you about the other happening. When you get time to set and let a feller tell you a story right and not have to jump in and tell it in as few words as possible, come back by. I ain't a-going to rush it like I did this'n.

Justice

IT seems to me if justice is done properly it ought to be done immediately after the deed. That way there can't be no pleasure took, which would be pay for doing it, nor remorse felt, which would be extra punishment. I never seen it happen that sudden but once.

Me and the two Nichols boys had been gathering cattle for Mr. Jordan up to Batson and had got through and stopped at Mr. J. G. Price's store to get some dinner on the way home. John Clendennin was there getting a bill of groceries and had a mule hooked to his wagon we hadn't none of us seen before. He'd drove up to where the mule's head was close to a big sweet-gum that growed close in front and had tied him to it with a piece of half-inch rope. We all knowed when we seen that that John had got a-holt of another outlaw. He was the dangdest feller I ever seen about buying or swapping for work stock that had been spoilt by mishandling, and trying to make them fit for using. We all set down on the front porch, and while we was eating our sardines and cheese and crackers, John told us about this black mule.

"I heard about that mule nearly killing a couple of men in the logging woods up to Saratoga, and rode up there to see about buying him. I located the feller that owned him, and he told me the mule could be bought for thirty dollars, which is less than half-price for a good mule, but any examining I done was at my own risk. Immediate I crawled over in the pen I knowed that mule had a special feeling for me from the way he come meeting me.

"I seen right off I couldn't stand all the affection that mule had for me, me being a bachelor and not used to it, so I just went right back over the fence. I was afeered I'd hurt his feelings by leaving so abrupt, but he'd got close enough to give me a little love bite and help hisself to a good portion of my shirt and seemed contented with that. After I'd got two or three fellers that was there a-watching to confirm that I wasn't bleeding too bad, I told the owner I'd buy that mule, that I believed I could give him the love and affection he seemed to have been deprived of. After I'd paid him, I got my whip off my saddle and climbed back in the pen, and time I hit the ground here come that mule again, ears laid back, head out, and them big teeth popping. I had come prepared with love and kisses of my own this time, though. I took a chunk out of that soft nose the first lick with that bullwhip and slowed him down and tried to take a ear off the next lick. Well, sir, that was two weeks ago, and I ain't never worked a better mule in my life than that one. Gentle, willing, and so sweet it's sickening, just a-biding his time till he can catch me off guard and kick my brains out. Ever' time something moves in back of him, be it fish, meat, or fowl, you can tell he just automatically calculates range, elevation, and windage. If either one of you boys is feeling bored with life, I'll be glad to swap you that mule. I guarantee he'll overcome that for you."

About then we heard a wagon coming and Big Nick stood up and looked and said it was Frank Pearson and his boy. Said Frank looked happy so he must have whipped his wife before he left home. This was just his way of passing an opinion on Frank Pearson, but it pegged the man to a T. He was the kind who kicks dogs, if they don't growl at him, whips and slaps his womenfolk around, if they don't threaten to take a skillet to him, and keeps his children scared half to death till they're half as big as him, but wouldn't say boo to a man if he spit in his face. By any measure, a bully. Mrs. Pearson had a ol' bachelor brother, lived in Houston, who'd tried to get her and the kids to come live with him, but she was so scared of Frank, said he'd kill her and the kids both, she wouldn't go. They had a little girl about four or five and the boy, about nine, that was with Frank. Frank was cussing and threatening the boy when he stopped the wagon and climbed down over a wheel.

All of us already had a bellyful of him, but when he howdied us we howdied back. None of us made a move till he turned around and seen the boy hadn't got down off the wagon and grabbed him and jerked the little feller like a bundle of fodder. When he done that, John Clendennin mumbled something about "another spoilt 'un" and reached and got his whip and started to get up. Little Nick was setting on the edge of the porch carving his initials in the floor, and I seen him close the little blade in his knife and open the big one, getting redder in the face all the time. It weren't setting a dang bit better with me and Big Nick than it was them, but we knowed either one of the two would kill Pearson if they ever started on him, and we didn't want it to go that far. I'd been setting by Little Nick and I just slid off the porch and pulled up a sleeve on my brush jumper and said how about him digging a black locust thorn out of my arm, since he had his knife out. About the same time Big Nick jerked a piece of binder twine out of his leggings pocket and ask' to see John's whip a minute so's he could twist a popper like was on it. Before Pearson had his team tied and him and the boy went in the store, I wished to hell Little Nick was cutting on him instead of me, mad as he was.

Big Nick had kept on at John Clendennin about that popper, and then slid his hands on up the whip and looked at the way it went from eight plait to four plait, and then gathered it in to where it went from sixteen plait to eight plait, and then went to admiring the way it was plaited on the stock, and Pearson went in just in time, Nick was dang near out of whip.

Well, it was about ten minutes before Pearson got his trading done and come out, and John and Little Nick had calmed down enough that I thought maybe he might get away before there was any trouble.

The boy came out first, toting a jug of kerosene and working on a stick of candy I knowed Mr. Price had give him. Frank come out right behind him with his arms full of groceries, and just as he went off the steps on the ground, he stepped on the boy's heel. 'Course the boy stumbled, and his daddy went to cussing and hollering watch where he was going and if he spilt that coal oil he'd take his hide off, and all of a sudden he just hauled off and kicked the boy with the inside of his boot. The young'un went sprawling in the side of John's wagon and dropped the jug and just stood there, about half stunned-like. Frank went to cussing louder and threatening worse and jumped and threw his armload in his wagon and went to pulling his belt off. About then he noticed the kerosene jug where it had rolled up behind John's black mule, and made for it, still raving and cussing. Just as he bent over to pick it up, John Clendennin's black mule reached back with his right hind foot and kicked Frank Pearson's damn brains out.

That was the finest example of justice I've ever seen.

The Big Fight at Old Man Kyser's

SURE, I remember that fight you're talking about. Happened at a dance at old man Kyser's house. I was there that night, and they tore down his whole front yard a-fighting with pickets. There was cypress splinters working out of me for two months afterwards. As far as I know, I'm the only man that knows that Bubba Hardin caused the whole mess the day he roped a alligator.

Me and him had both been out of the army about two months and was doing what they called "re-adjusting" back then. This mainly consisted of laying around on our behinds and doing what the hell ever we wanted to do. I think now they call it "doing your own thing."

Anyway, this particular day we'd rode over 'crost Green's Bayou to the river, not up to anything special, just riding and looking, and just as we rode out on that long sandbar between Moore's Lake and the river, we seen a pretty good little gator, maybe four and a half or five feet long, heading acrost the bar towards Moore's Lake. Bubba fetched a whoop and lit out for him, getting his rope down. He was riding a ol' tall rawboney mare that'd come off a racetrack over in Louisiana somewhere. Whichever way she was headed when she started was the way you went long's the ride lasted. Well, sir, he had her headed right, and just before that gator got off the bar, they passed behind him and Bubba snared the little feller. Like most hands in this Big Thicket country, he had his rope tied hard and fast to his foretree, and time they got to the end of that thirty-foot manila, he'd iron-handed that mare to a stop, swapped ends with her, and had her looking down that rope like a roping hoss, and was looking so proud of hisself he couldn't stand it.

In case you never roped a gator, I better explain what they do. They ain't like a cow or hoss or most anything else on a rope, pulling and running sidewards; they go to rolling over and over, which is what this'n done, and ever' time he rolled he shortened Bubba's rope and got closer, and danged if I didn't think he was going to climb in the saddle with him! That ol' fool mare was a-walling her eyes and shaking all over, and about the time that gator got in eight or ten foot of her, she couldn't stand no more and wheeled and left there. She went up over the river bank and headed east. Bubba was snatching his reins right and left, but he might as well been pulling on a snubbing post, right through them bad briers and vines at the head of Moore's Lake. I still don't know how he rode that stampeding animal through there, but when she got to Black Pond, maybe four, five hundred yards from the river, he was still with her. I was riding hard as I could, but I never got no closer than to see that little gator bounce ever' once in a while. I just knowed they'd went around the edge of Black Pond and was still a-going, but when I popped out of the brush, there was that danged gator laying belly up and Bubba and that crazy mare about twenty foot out from the bank. It'd been a pretty dry year and the pond wasn't much more than a mud-hole, and she's bogged slam to the point of her shoulders. Time I got off my horse, Bubba got off her and come wallering towards the bank, and I got his rope off that gator and slung the little feller back up in the briers. I knowed he'd get blamed for the wreck and figured he'd be safer there.

I tell you, I've seen men go through some fracases, but I ain't never seen one look bad as Bubba did. Muddy, bloody

The Big Fight at Old Man Kyser's

as a fresh cowhide, no shirt, no hat, scratched up like he'd just changed a tomcat freehand, both knees nearly broke from hitting against trees, and mud and blood squirting out of a big cut on a boot where a bamboo brier had drug across it. If I'd of been armed, I believe I'd have shot him to get him out of his misery.

Anyway, whilst he laid down a few minutes, I throwed my rope over his mare's head and tried to help her to get out, but I seen pretty quick she's bogged too bad and we'd have to get something under her. Well, Bubba was too beat up to help, and that didn't leave nobody but me, so I gathered up all the chunks and limbs that was handy and tied his rope around them so's I could drag 'em, and shucked my boots and britches and wallered out and went to pushing that stuff under her. I seen right off I didn't have enough, so I told Bubba to get on my horse and drag some more in. About the time he started to ride off I says, "Now be dang sure not to rope nothing that looks like a alligator." Well, sir, I've heard them skinners in France bless out them mules they hauled over there, but I ain't never heard cussing like Bubba used on me. It did seem to cheer him up considerable, though, and him and my little brown pretty soon had a good pile of chunks ready for me, and I'd got the mare turned around and heading towards the bank. It was mighty slow, though, and Bubba finally got in there with me, but even with both of us it took maybe two hours. I don't reckon I ever spent two more miserable hours in my life. Wallering around in that mud with the sun beaming down and not a breath of air stirring and the dang mosquitoes and buffalo gnats eating us up and just for variety ever' once in a while a greenhead or deerfly would pop it to us. When we finally got that damn mare to hard ground I was so proud I'd have cried if it hadn't been for the tears streaking my mud shirt.

I didn't think she could make it home after that trial, but after we'd went to the river and washed her down and cleaned ourselves up we headed for home, taking our time, and she finally made it in with Bubba.

'Course I told it on him and he took a lot of hoorawing about roping the gator, but I didn't know it was working on him bad as it was till that night at old man Kyser's dance.

There was some folks named Blake lived here then, and they had four old boys from about seventeen to twenty-two or three, and one mighty pretty girl along in there somewhere, Cerola her name was, and Bubba had been sparking her a good while and brought her to the dance that night. 'Course him being sweet on her like he was, he didn't like anybody else dancing with her, and we'd been deviling him all night asking her to dance and cutting in and such, and he's getting pretty cloudy and about ready to jump the first one that give him a reason to.

Well, sir, I guess I was the one that finally touched him off. I'd danced with Cerola the set before and I'd told her that Bubba knew a new dance called the Alligator Drag and she ought to get him to teach it to her. Well, she danced the next time with him, and right after the music stopped and it's over, she says, "Oh, Bubba, would you show me how you do the Alligator Drag?" I 'spect if the high sheriff had of been the closest man, that's who he'd of hit, but Cerola's brother Franklin was, and that's who he set the hair on. I don't know if their folks told them to do it or not, but you could bet that wherever Cerola was, her four brothers was standing close around, and Bubba hadn't no more than hit Franklin when one of the others, Basil, I believe it was, hung one on him. Well, sir, ol' Basil wound up right square in front of me, and before I thought, I just laid him out. About then Mr. Kyser went to hollering, "Get outside, boys, and fight all you want, but you'll not fight in my house without answering to me." Well, we all knowed the old man didn't bluff, and there weren't nothing to do but get outside, and the upshot was two or three more fights in the front yard. Then somebody jerked one of them cypress pickets off the fence and rapped somebody else with it, and then ever'body went to doing it. Time it was over, there weren't nothing left of that nice picket fence but kindling.

And that's the way a danged little ol' alligator caused the big fight at old man Kyser's dance.

A Twenty-Four-Hour, Seven-Days-a-Week Preacher

IT would be hard for me to say whether or not a man would be a better preacher if he were educated for it, but I expect he would be if he were the right kind of a man to begin with. I never knowed but two preachers whilst I was church-going, one educated one and old Brother Cass Elliott.

Brother Cass was, as old Mrs. Lyrock said it, pasturing our church as far back as I remember, and I expect most of his book learning come from McGuffy's Reader and a blue-back speller. Time I got up far enough to remember, he'd been at the Book so much he didn't need to read, just quoted word for word. 'Course back then there wasn't all this literature to read in church like now. Just the Bible.

Brother Cass appeared to be a fool in lots of ways, especially to us ol' knotheaded boys, but after I was grown I realized how slick he was about getting us to set up and listen in church. We was shooting marbles at school during lunch hour once, and he come by on his mule and got down and borrowed two peyakers for stakes and a alley for a shooter and knuckled down with us and done just pretty durn good. 'Course, like most men middle-age or past, he was telling us how good he used to be and how fast he could run when he was a young feller and wound up telling us about a preacher he knowed back then. Said he always started his sermons at Genesis and worked his way book by book till he fell off the end of Revelations. And him and the other boys would bet marbles and tops and things with each other on what book, chapter, and verse certain men in the congregation would go to sleep on and which one they'd wake up on.

Well, you know, boys, it weren't long till we'd noticed Brother Cass laid out his sermons the same way he said this other preacher done, and from then on we couldn't wait to get to church Sunday mornings to get some bets down. We was just some tickled that we was putting one over on him.

Now I know this sounds like bad goings on, especially in church, but if you've ever set through a two- or three-hour sermon when you was a kid and not interested, you know how tedious and boring it is, fighting to stay awake and be still so's your Ma or Pa wouldn't bust you afterwards, and probably some old feller closer to needing the words than you setting there head up and sound asleep.

Some men get to talking and just like the sound of their voice so much seems like they ain't never going to quit, but I've got to give Brother Cass credit. He always preached a long time, but it weren't because he was listening to Cass. No, he was just searching for the right words to bring some sinner down that aisle, and he was always so sure he was close that he just couldn't bear to quit. That little game he let slip to us boys kept us watching so close to see what we'd won or lost that we didn't do much sleeping or squirming from then on. And I'll tell you something else, after nearly fifty years I can still name the books in both testaments in rotation, tell you how many chapters in each book, how many verses in each chapter. And it still surprises me how much I remember besides that.

Brother Cass weren't one to just work at his trade on Sundays and Wednesday prayer-meeting, either. No, sir, Brother Cass was a twenty-four-hour, seven-days-a-week man when needed. 'Course, there not being any hospitals then, all the sick was nursed at home. You could figure on

A Twenty-Four-Hour, Seven-Days-a-Week Preacher

him being there ever' night he was needed to set up. The dead weren't turned over to no strangers then, neither, but were kept at home till they was put in the ground. That old feller set with a corpse many a long night with his head bowed praying for the family. He didn't stop his work after he'd helped with the afflictions and spiritual needs of his flock, either, but just pulled off his good clothes and got on his overalls and helped with the ever'day labor. 'Course, if he could combine the two, he'd work both at the same time.

I remember one morning we was fixing to go to the field to hoe corn, and he come riding up and went to unsaddling his mule and told Papa, "Brother Gray, I noticed the bermuder grass has sure got bad in your corn since it rained, and I've always considered bermuder a instrument of the devil; if you don't mind, I'll just go along with y'all and get a few licks at him." Well, we all knowed that grass was in for a bad time because Brother Cass hoed like he was fighting yellow-jackets. But we also knowed Pa's old bachelor brother that lived with us was fixing to get a few licks about his drinking, too. Well, sir, us boys laughed about Uncle Beau for a week after that. We all stopped on the turn-row and sharpened our hoes, and Uncle Beau took two rows and Brother Cass took the next two and then me two, and Little Beau and Jody—they was only about nine and ten then—they carried one apiece. Uncle Beau got sharpened up first and went to chopping grass and thinning corn hard as he could so's to get way ahead of that preacher, but us boys had been in the field with him before and knowed ol' Beau wasn't going to make it. Directly Brother Cass got ready and here he went after Uncle Beau like the devil beating tanbark, as the old saying goes. Well, in about twenty yards he'd done caught up with ol' Uncle Beau, so Beau just slowed down and was gonna let him get on out ahead. But

Brother Cass never slowed his hoeing a bit. Just reached over and went to hoeing the nearest one of Beau's rows and stayed about a step behind. Uncle Beau was bad as us boys about wearing shoes, and we was all barefooted that morning. He was sure acting flinchy with that preacher hacking and slashing right alongside his feet.

About halfway to the other end, Brother Cass says, "Beauregard, I hear your drinking problem has cropped up again."

Well, he was wrong there. *Getting* it was Uncle Beau's problem, drinking it sure weren't.

Anyways, Beau says, "Elliott, I ain't a member—be a little more careful with that sharp hoe, there, Cass—of your church and it—slow down a little, Preacher, that corn's done jointed and won't come back out—ain't none of your business—you ain't killing snakes, Brother Cass, don't chop quite so far this way—how much I drink. Reverend Elliott, if you'll just let me get out of reach of that durn hoe I'll try hard as I can not to drink anymore!"

Uncle Beau's drouth just lasted about a month, but far's I know, it was a record for him.

Another thing Brother Cass done was keep many a man in the field working when he was sick enough to be in bed. They knowed if they took to their bed, when the neighbors come to work their crop out, Brother Cass would be there with his mule to help and what them two could do to a cornfield was something. Uncle Beau claimed he seen them just ride by a field of young corn once and the leaves rolled up on two acres of it. He was sober at the time, though, so nobody really believed it.

Most men kept a kind of wire muzzle on their work stock when they was plowing corn so's the animal wouldn't be biting the tops out, but Brother Cass didn't believe in "muzzling the ox that treadeth out the grain," so he never put one on ol' Rhody.

When they turned off the turn-row to start plowing, Brother Cass always stopped and spit on his hands whilst Rhody gathered in a mouthful of corn, and then he'd slap him with his lines and tell him, "Git up there, Rhody, and let's give the Lord a good day's work," and the race was on. Well, sir, old Rhody was a long-walking mule anyway and weighed about twelve hundred, big for this country, and they'd go down a middle faster'n a diving bull-bat, and about ever' ten foot Brother Cass would turn loose of one plow handle and slap Rhody with them lines and holler, "Hup, there, Rhody," and ever' time he done that he'd let his plow run sidewards and get three, four stalks of corn and about ever' "Hup," ol' Rhody'd get him three or four more stalks. Time they got through a cornpatch it'd look like somebody planted for half a stand and got it.

Well, you can see the old feller weren't perfect, but we all knowed how good his intentions was and he just suited us. But directly the railroad come through and the country went to settling up and our church got to wanting a neater, nicer preacher than him. 'Course they laid it out that after forty years he needed a rest and he'd live longer for it and it was for his own good, but that didn't make it any easier on Brother Cass.

Finally, though, he decided that maybe it was the Lord's will that he step down. He accepted it, and me and him both quit the same night. I think most folks kinda regretted it and felt maybe a little low-down about forcing him out after they'd done it, but the old feller died a couple of months later, and knowing they wouldn't have to ever face him again helped their feelings a lot.

Well, they hired another preacher pretty quick after

they got rid of Brother Cass, a young feller just out of some school, and he just fell in and organized things and had business meetings and got most ever'body on a committee of some kind or other, and worked so hard it kept a woman busy full time starching and ironing his shirts. Folks was mighty well pleased with him for six or eight months, but then he run off with a married woman and left a pore dang log-hauler to raise three young'uns with no mother.

A man would be a fool if he couldn't see that educating a man for the job would help him be a better preacher, just like he'd be a fool if he couldn't see bricks would build a better house than logs. But, house or man, if you ain't got a good foundation to build on you've wasted your time.

Horse Trading

SURE, there used to be horse traders come through this country often. Some of 'em regular, some just now and then. One I remember, feller named Clyde Dillon, come through ever' year about the same time. Pa said the first time he remembered him was 1920, and he never missed a year till 1938. I don't know whether he died, quit trading, or just went some other route, but 1937 was the last time he come here.

He always had a wagon and was leading or driving anywhere from ten, twelve, to maybe thirty head of horses and mules, and he'd camp under a big gum tree across in front of Pa's place about a quarter, usually about a week or ten days, and ride out over the country till folks got the news he was here. After that he mostly stayed in camp, and them that had trading stock or needed to buy an animal would come there to do their business.

I've heard lots of bad tales about horse traders and the way they'd hook folks in a trade, but they weren't much worse than lots of businessmen. Most people that got beat in a horse trade was out to beat them and just got out-traded, and was fools to start with. Trading was something the average man seldom done, and them old traders done it ever' day and a man was crazy to try to trade anyway but honest.

I remember once there was a feller lived just below us, McWaters I believe his name was, weren't here long, had a helluva good looking sorrel horse that was just a little bit heavey. Not much, just when it was hot and dry he'd heave some, and Mr. McWaters set in to trade him to Clyde Dillon.

Well, they finally struck a bargain and McWaters come out of it with a little snakey black pony that was probably a good horse in his day, which was several years in his past, and stopped by the house to show him to Pa and was bragging big about how he stuck Dillon with the sorrel.

Well, sir, a couple of weeks later I'd took some corn to the gristmill at Walter. It was regular grinding day and there was several men and boys there, McWaters among them, a-waiting for their corn to be ground, and Clyde Dillon rode up. Before he got his horse stopped good, McWaters stepped forward and sung out, "Get off that horse, Dillon, I'm goin' to whip you till you wished you'd been born a girl-child."

Well, now any fool would have knowed Dillon hadn't traveled and traded all over this Big Thicket country amongst men that was rougher and tougher than the back hide on a ten-foot gator without being able to stand up for hisself, but from the soft way he answered back, you'd have thought he was mild as store-bought soap.

"I don't believe I'll take you up on that offer, Mr. Mc-Waters," he says, "since I've already had a better one this morning. Mr. Smith just now offered to take me off this horse and do the same thing. Even so, sir, I would like to know why you're riled at me."

"You know why," McWaters says. "That black you traded me has got the heaves."

"Why, so he has," Dillon says, "and so has the sorrel you traded me. I would have mentioned about the black, but you said you'd owned the sorrel ten years and I figured after that long you was a expert on heavey horses."

Ever'body there could see it was time for McWaters to shut up, 'cept McWaters. "Well," he says, "you knowed I wanted that black to hunt on and you outright lied when you said I could shoot off him. I've fired a gun on him twice and he's went crazy and danged near throwed me down both times."

"No, no," says Dillon, "I didn't lie about that. You misunderstood. I certainly did say you could shoot off him, but what I meant was you'd dang sure *better be off him* when you shoot!"

Now, I don't mean them old-time traders weren't out to make a profit. They had to do that to make a living. What I'm trying to show is that the ones like Clyde Dillon wouldn't hook a man that come to them trading open and honest, but would try to send him off with a good sound animal of the type he needed. Several times over the years I seen Dillon tell some feller that a certain horse wasn't what he was looking for and sell him a cheaper one and he'd be perfectly satisfied. I've also seen him trade back a few times when a feller wasn't too well suited with what he'd got, but generally speaking, a trade was a trade and was held to.

Lots of people nowadays has read and heard so many of them old yarns about people getting hooked with unsound animals that they think there weren't never no good horses or mules traded. That's not even close to the truth. Lots of times a man would need a bigger or better team, maybe he'd got young'uns up big enough to help in the field and was taking in more land, or maybe some other reason, and would have a good, sound light team to trade in. Or maybe it was the other way, and his children had left home and he had a pair of good heavy horses to trade down to a lighter team. There was any number of reasons a feller might trade off a sound animal. 'Course, with some fellers trading was a fever like gambling and they traded regular, looking for a horse that perfect suited them, I guess, and usually swapped theirself afoot pretty often.

No, all stock that was traded weren't windbroke or

spavined or diseased, no more than all horse traders was crooked. I always figured them old fellers done a real service, moving horses and mules back and forth to where they was needed most, and they sure wouldn't have made close to the same route ever' year if they'd wore out their welcome by too sharp trading.

You know, that run-in Dillon and McWaters had reminds me of another yarn. They use to call a good milk cow a family cow because she'd give enough milk for a whole family. Well, they told on old man Blakeley, up to Grand Cane, that he bought a big ol' longhorn cow from a feller for a family cow, and the next day he was back at that feller's house madder'n hell, wanting to know how come that feller tell him she was a family cow. Says he started to milk her and she fought so bad it took him and his wife and all five kids to get her tied to the fence and her hind legs tied together, and then she didn't give but a quart of milk.

"Mr. Blakeley," this feller says, "that's what I meant by family cow. It takes the whole damn family to milk her."

The Killings

OH, sure, there's been lots of killings in this country. Especially during the oil-boom days at Batson and Saratoga. Old Milvid and Mary C. and the other logging camps had their share during their heyday, too. I don't recollect but three, maybe four, right here at home, though.

Let's see, now, Dan Thomas killed a feller, a Mexican. I heard his name at the time but I've forgot it. Mr. Kroger killed Dr. Banning. Fletcher Morrow killed a feller name of Baines, and Mr. George Redding killed O. R. Manning. Them four is all I remember offhand.

There wasn't none of them killings done during no shoot-out. I never heard of one in this country. These was more or less executions. Seemed like around here when a man figured another one needed killing he went at it like any other job, picked the best tool for it and got it over with.

Dr. Banning and Baines was both killed with the same ol' double-barrel Remington ten-gauge. I think maybe some of the Krogers still own it. George Redding used a old Winchester lever-action ten-gauge on Mr. Manning. Papa said it was the best shooting shotgun he'd ever seen and had killed a million ducks and geese when Mr. Redding was market-hunting. I don't know what ever happened to it.

Dan Thomas killed the Mexican with a old .41 single-action Colt pistol. It was more or less a case of have to, and Dan would have got out of it if he could have. He was constable in this precinct then, he weren't no gun-toter like some lawmen, just farmed and worked out when he could, like most folks. He only run for the job because the county paid five dollars a month regular and fees for serving papers and such.

That shooting come about when the police at Houston sent Dan a telegram that this Mexican feller had knifed a man and was on a freight train heading this way. Dan had the station agent flag the train and was searching it when the Mexican made at him with that knife, and Dan put a ball in his forehead. I 'spect that shot was an accident. Dan didn't shoot that much.

Fletch Morrow claimed at his trial he'd killed Baines because he'd feared for his life. Told on the stand that they'd had words over some of Baines' hogs tearing in his field, and Baines said next time he seen him he was going to kill him if he got life in the pen for it. Two or three days after they'd had the words, Fletcher seen him pass on the road to town and was behind a tree waiting for him when he come back. One of the Carr kids was coming from the gristmill and seen it, and he said Fletcher shot Baines once while he was walking and again before he hit the ground.

Old man Kroger set in a saloon and waited for Dr. Banning and shot him when he stepped in the door. I heard several tales, but it was four or five years before I heard the straight of the matter, and then I wished I hadn't. It was personal between the two men and none of my business. Nor yours. They've both still got folks living around here.

I knowed a little more than just second- or third-hand talk about Mr. Redding killing Mr. Manning. They was both close neighbors of ours. Papa had a place then about seven miles out of Liberty on the old Nacodoches stage road, and Mr. Redding lived about half a mile below us, what they call the Bob Ray place now. Mr. Manning was farming the Hardin place on up above us about a mile.

Well, their falling out was about a dog and come up this way. Papa and Mr. Manning went one morning to George Redding's to help butcher hogs, and when they started into the yard one of Mr. Redding's dogs bit Mr. Manning. Papa said since they were expected, neither one of them had hollered hello nor spoke to the dog before they opened the gate, so he kinda figured the dog was in the right.

After dinner Mr. Manning was cutting up a hog—they was working in the backyard so's the well was handy—and the old dog came in under the table and bit him again. Papa said he could tell it really set him afire that time, but he just said if he had a biting dog he'd break his damn jaw, and kept on a-working.

A few days later the dog come in home with his bottom jaw busted in three or four places. Not being able to eat or drink, 'course he didn't pull through. Mr. Redding was sure mad and looking for somebody to put the blame on, and the upshot was he accused Mr. Manning of killing his dog. Mr. Manning denied it, and one word led to another, and they was both pretty hot before it was over.

Now, you understand, this weren't just no pet dog. This was a cur dog like most folks in this country kept and as necessary as a plow or axe or any other tool. There just weren't no way a feller could tend to hogs or gather cattle in this Big Thicket country without dogs, and can't till yet.

A man's got a natural feeling for his own dog anyhow, and when it's a using dog and they work together a few years, he also develops a kind of respect for the dog and don't like to have him bad-mouthed and ain't going to have him hurt or abused. I've always figured Mr. Redding felt that way about his old dog.

Well, things rocked on awhile, and ever'body got busy

putting their crops in, and it looked like it had blowed over about the dog till along in June.

A feller had moved in on the Christian place that winter, about three miles east of us, and had got in twelve or fifteen acres of corn and a patch of sweet taters and then got down with recurrent fever. It was really malaria, but we didn't know it as such at that time. Anyway, Mama heard at church one Sunday that folks was going to work his crop Tuesday, if it didn't rain.

Well, the weather stayed clear and we was pretty well out of the grass at home, so Tuesday morning me and Papa loaded up some plow tools on the wagon and got ourself over there about sun-up. There was about nine or ten men showed up. Mr. Redding and Mr. Manning both come, and maybe as many boys.

Mr. Will Martin, this feller's closest neighbor, kinda took over and sorted ever'body out as to what to do. (I thought that feller's name would come to me in a minute, but I be dang if I can recollect it.) Well, anyway, the feller's woodpile was so low his wife was picking up chips, so Mr. Will told off three or four men and some boys to tend to wood-getting and put the rest of us to hoeing or plowing.

Papa got out some coffee Mama had ground and sent by us, and the man's wife built a fire around her washpot in the backyard and kept hot coffee for us all day. She'd of fed us, too, such as they had, but we'd all brought a lunch, mostly biscuits and bacon and syrup or jelly, packed in a syrup bucket to keep out dirt and ants and such.

'Long about the middle of the day the fellers getting wood come in with a couple of good loads of blocks, and we all spread our grub out along the edge of the back porch and got some of that hot coffee and had us a syrup-bucket banquet. 'Course we insisted the feller's wife and kids eat something. The lady just eat a few bites here and there, just enough so she could say how good it tasted and how well it was cooked, but them three little young'uns didn't just nibble. They'd been on sawmill gravy and cornbread and garden sass so long they sure did wade into them biscuits and sweet'nin' and sidemeat. After they ate till their navels was sticking out like a pot leg, I seen Mr. Redding open his syrup bucket and take out a piece of cake he'd saved back and go divide it amongst the three. Time we went back to work, their ma had throwed a quilt down in the dog trot where it was cool, and them little fellers was piled up like puppies and dead to the world.

Shorty Lloyd was there a-helping that day. Shorty was the kind of feller that always had a funny story to tell. Whilst we was eating he got to telling us about a Watkins Products peddler walking into old Mrs. Smith's yard and before she could get to the door and holler one of her dogs took a britches leg off for him. Said the peddler told him he believed the dog would have got the other one, but he kept dodging and kicking till he got in a good lick and knocked him down.

Mr. Manning spoke up and said he'd of stomped his damn head off while he had him down. When he said that, I seen George Redding wheel and give him a hard look, and I knowed then things hadn't blowed over as much as I thought.

Well, we'd got through hoeing that morning, so us that'd been at that helped split and stack the wood and the men got back to plowing, and by three or four o'clock we was all finished, loaded up, and ready to go home.

To show you how folks neighbored them days, Mr. Will Martin had broke a plow handle that morning and the rest of the day he'd used a old Georgia Stock that belonged to the feller where we was working. (What in the hell was that feller's name? All I can think of is Jackson, and I know dang well that ain't it.) Well, anyway, this feller couldn't get out of bed, but Mr. Will made it a point to go in ever' once in awhile and ask about something or get his advice about what we was doing and ever' time he did he'd brag on that old plow. Easiest running plow he'd ever seen and the best handling and I don't know what all. That evening he told the feller he was going to butcher a beef the next day, and if he could spare that Georgia Stock, he'd swap him a forequarter for it. 'Course, they both knowed that old plow wasn't worth half what the beef was, but Mr. Will knowed the feller wouldn't take the beef as a outright gift, bad as he needed it. By swapping this way, it was changed from just plain charity and he got to keep a little pride and got the beef for his family too.

After the kids went to sleep, the lady—(that feller's name was Grayson, Albert Gray—no, Elbert Grayson. I knowed I'd recollect it after a while).

Well, as I was saying, after the kids went to sleep Mrs. Grayson had went and gathered a bunch of garden sass and had it all washed and cleaned, and after we was loaded up and ready to go, she invited the men to help themselves, if they needed any of it. 'Course they had plenty of such at home, but they all picked out a mess of something and made over it and said how nice the stuff was. Papa took a bunch of mustard greens and said he was proud to get them, that the lice had took ours, which was a lie, and Shorty Lloyd took a big handful of radishes and said he was glad to get the damn things, that he believed ever' damn radish his wife had planted the whole damn year had been pithy by the time they come up, and he hadn't had a decent damn radish for two damn months. Shorty was good-hearted but had been knowed to cuss. Mr. Manning took some tomatoes and said theirs

The Killings 83

was late and they hadn't had one all spring the worms hadn't been at, and thanked her two or three times, and the rest done about the same.

I 'spect the lady knew they had plenty of such truck at home, but it was all she had to offer for what we'd done and them men weren't about to shame her by belittling it. Helping folks when they need it is fine and is highly spoke of in the Good Book, but if it ain't done in such a way that they can hold their heads up afterwards it's best not done at all.

You could tell ever'body felt good about the day's work from the way they was laughing and joshing when we pulled out for home. They also knowed their neighboring would be paid back if they ever needed it.

Papa and me went by Mr. Manning's and helped him block his wagon up so's he could pull the wheels and grease the spindles. Whilst we was at it, I heard him tell Papa he was going to meet the road gang at Woods Spring the next morning and finish working out his road tax. Back then you could pay it in money or work it out three days a year.

The next morning a little after good daylight, me and Papa had finished feeding and was going to the house after more coffee when Mr. Manning passed and waved at us. He was riding at a lope, and Papa remarked he'd got off late.

About the time Mama brought our coffee out on the front porch, we heard a shot, and in a minute or two another one. We could tell they was about at Mr. Redding's, and in just another minute or two we heard Mrs. Redding scream, just as clear. Me and Mama and Papa all three started running that way hard as we could. I wouldn't have believed it, but Papa outrun me and met Mrs. Redding first, about halfway to their place, and shook her till she quit screaming and told him George had killed Mr. Manning. When I got to them, he told me to take her back to meet Mama and help get her to our house and then catch my saddle horse and meet him at Redding's, that I'd have to go to Liberty for the sheriff.

Mr. Redding had stood at his front gate with that old ten-gauge and shot Mr. Manning off his horse and then walked out to the road and shot him again point-blank.

Papa always said them two was the best men he'd ever neighbored with.

Just Talking

YEP, they finally got Uncle Jube to go to church last week. I ask' him how long it'd been since he'd darkened the door on one, and he said he didn't rightly recollect, said he'd went two Sundays in a row right after he'd married and it seemed like to him he'd been married forever. Aunt Martha said it'd been fifty-three years this fall. Uncle Jube allowed he wouldn't have minded going another time or two, that he'd noticed several people taking naps and looking powerful comfortable, but he couldn't abide foolishness and that's what the preacher seemed set on talking.

Seems the first Sunday they was having a little dry spell, and this preacher announced he was going to pray for rain and would git it, too, if the devil didn't keep it away. Uncle Jube said any fool knowed if he'd just prayed up a three-day east wind he'd been sure of rain, devil or no, because when the wind stayed out of the east that long in this country all hell couldn't keep it from raining. Said he didn't intend to go no more. But he'd always considered hisself a fair-minded man, and that week it struck him that maybe this preacher hadn't been living in Southeast Texas long and didn't know the variables of what passed for weather around here, and he concluded he'd give him one more chance. Well, sir, according to Uncle Jubal it was worse the next Sunday. Said the preacher told them he was starting a seven-day revival the following Sunday and when it was over he intended for ever'body in the sound of his voice to be ready to cross the River Jordan. Uncle Jube said he didn't know that river but figured since the preacher wasn't raised here he might of miscalled the Trinity or may the Sabine, and decided if he had his corn pulled by then, he'd just go along with the rest and catfish awhile after the crossing. Said he believed he'd of made the trip, too, if that preacher'd quit talking right then, but he kept on, and before it was over, he'd told them he knew he'd have ever' lamb found and brought in at the end of that revival. Uncle Jube said that capped it far as he's concerned, said he knew that preacher's home place and there weren't more'n four acres in it and he didn't have but six sheep and two lambs, and he wasn't going to have a man that needed seven days to find two lambs in a four-acre patch rafting him across no dang river.

I should of had more sense than that preacher and shut up whilst I was ahead, but no, I had to ask the old man about this last trip.

"Well, sir," he says, "it was a little more enlighting than the other two. I don't believe it were the same preacher, but this'n's ideas was about the same. Seemed to have sin on his mind a lot, and judging from the way he talked, seemed to be agin it. I'd decided I'd get comfortable and go to sleep like them other folks soon as I could, but before I got set down good, he kinda drawed hisself up and looked us all right in the eye and said his text fer the day would be the Prodigal Son. Well, sir, I listened close the whole time he was talking, and I never was plumb sure whether that was the feller's name or whether he was describing him and, being a preacher, wouldn't say the rest of it. Anyway, he told about this young feller's papa outfitting him with a good horse and saddle and a pocketful of money and fine clothes and letting him leave home to make his own way.

"Course, being a boy, he didn't hardly get out of sight of home before he was drinking some, maybe gambling a little, and chasing the girls. That was predictable, being the way of young fellers, and his papa probably knew a man ain't got work on his mind when he leaves home in a blue serge suit, and allowed enough extra for it, but before the boy got his wild oats sowed and settled down to work somebody caught him drunk and robbed him of that roll he'd been flashing around town and stole his suit and horse and saddle. When he sobered up broke, naked, and afoot, there weren't nothing for him to do but beg a ol' wore-out saddle blanket to wear and get his foot in his hand and head for home. He musta had a good ways to travel, for he was so durn hungry by the time he got in sight of the home place he fell over in the hog pen and went to the trough. I expect being awful ashamed to face his family had something to do with that. I'd about decided that I knowed that feller till the preacher told that one. Mr. Rowe over on Marcel Prairie got a-holt of some oil money a few years back, and it had sounded a lot like a stunt one of his boys pulled. I knowed, though, when he told that about the hog pen that it sure didn't happen in this country. If he'd got in the pen with these razorbacks we got in this Big Thicket country, he wouldn't of ate, he'd of got ate. Anyways, he wound up telling about his papa finding the boy and making him go to the creek and wash up and giving him some decent clothes and barbecuing a fat calf and having a big dance and doing for him and saying he didn't give a durn if the boy had swapped his birthday for a mess of partridge, he was still his son. I expect this was mostly done and said in front of the neighbors, though, and the boy heard a different story in private."

About then Aunt Martha spoke up and says, "Jubal, you quit putting that boy on. He'll think you're the biggest fool in the world."

"Martha," he says, "the bigger fool he thinks I am, the better trade I can make for that new barlow knife he's a-whittling with."

Yessir, that's Uncle Jube out and out.

Courting

It was forty years ago the first time I ever got serious over a girl, but I ain't never forgot what I went through a-courting her. She was one of old man Joe Brocker's girls and I'd been knowing her all her life, but it seemed like she just growed up overnight and the first I knowed she was a grown woman pretty as twin colts. I was about twenty, and like most fellers that age with the sweets on a girl, I was hanging around her ever' minute I could and going through hell wanting to be there the rest of the time. It was a good seven miles from our place to Mr. Brocker's, and I sure did use up the horse flesh going back and forth. Papa had five or six head of good saddle horses, but they was used to help make a living and he weren't even about to let me use one to do my sparking, so I generally rode something I was breaking for somebody or some spoilt, half-outlawed fool I'd swapped for. Seems like I best remember the hurry I stayed in them days. I'd hurry all day to do all I could so maybe Papa would let me off a little early, hurry to eat supper so I could hurry to clean up so I could hurry to get on the road to Mr. Brocker's (while I was there time done the hurrying for me), and then hurry to get home so's I could get some sleep before Papa rousted us out. Like most of them old-timers, if he had a suspicion daylight was gonna come, he had you up an hour beforehand ready to greet it.

Well, sir, I don't know how many scrapes I got into during that time with them fool horses. The first time, I was coming in one night riding a little ol' half bridle-wise horse I was breaking, and just before I got home one of our dogs come out of the road ditch and jumped up against my leg and barked, and that dang horse throwed me the length of the bridle rein before I knowed what was happening. Another time I was riding a horse I'd traded for, a helluva good-looking animal them Statens down towards Cedar Bayou had raised. He was a good horse, too, long as you was working in a pen or just riding along, but anytime you got faster than a slow lope then you was going horseback riding! You could generally stop him after a couple of miles, but the next time you jumped him off it was the same thing. Well, I was coming in on him that night, so sleepy both eyes was blinking out of the same hole, and about two miles from home I figured I'd just jump him off and let him get me home in a hurry, and he'd be blowed up time I got there and I could stop him. The road was dirt but it was maintained by the county and reasonably straight and fairly smooth, and even though there weren't any moon, I figured I could see good enough to go around if there was anything on it. I was about as far wrong as a feller could be. I want you to know, mister, when I pushed my bridle reins at that old pony and kicked him, we did leave there. We hadn't gone a quarter before the wind had my eyes watering so bad I couldn't see nothing, all I could do was drop my hat brim and ride. Man, I tell you, we was going home like a goose riding south on a cold norther and was halfway there when a big cow riz up in front of ol' cold-jaw, and he hit her broadside! Far as I know there could have been a hundred cows bedded down in the road there, but I never took note of but three. The one he hit, the one I landed on right after me and him parted company, and the one I lit on after I fell off of that'n. I hit belly down on the first, and you could have heard me grunt clear to the house when the breath left me. When I slid on over that'n, I fell between the horns on the other'n and hung there a second and then fell off and she run over me, but the first one I'd been on had me to where I wasn't 'specially interested in what this'n done. I was lucky and didn't get no broke bones out of it, and my ol' horse was just stove up about a week, but me and him both learnt something. I ain't never stayed with a runaway horse since then, and far as I know that was the last time he ever cold-jawed.

The next scrape was more embarrassing than anything else. I was breaking a young horse for a Mr. Hamshire that lived in town, and one Saturday after dinner I rode him since I had plenty of time. Them days we didn't generally break a horse till he was four, but this one was a good bred Morgan and big enough time he was two, and Mr. Hamshire was paying me five dollars to take my time and do a good job. Well, sir, Mr. Brocker had recent built him a yard fence out of split-cypress pickets, and that evening when I got there I just dropped my reins over three or four of them pickets and went on in. I knowed that colt was shedding his colt teeth and cutting his permanent ones and was chewing sticks and corn cobs and anything else rough he could get in his mouth trying to relieve them sore gums, but it never crossed my mind he'd bother them pickets. I thought about it when I come out to go home just before dark, though. That son-of-a-bitch had eat three, four inches off the tops of them soft cypress pickets far as the bridle reins let him reach both sides! I got out of that one easy by paying one of my girl's brothers fifty cents to fix the fence.

The next wreck I got into was bad but could have been worse. That fourteen miles I was riding to Mr. Brocker's and back was getting longer and longer riding them fool horses, so when Clyde Dillon come through that summer trading horses, I swapped him out of a bald-faced sorrel that had a good, smooth foxtrot and figured I had my transportation problem whipped. Old Bald was a road horse all right, and nine times out of ten you rode him he was steady and reliable, but ever' once in a while he'd be snorty and looking for boogers and you had to watch him ever' second or he'd get out from under you and go home with your saddle. Papa always said he'd got nearsighted from some cause or other when he got like that. Anyway, he'd been acting like that all the way to Mr. Brocker's the evening this happened, and I was plumb ready to get off him time we got there. I knowed he wasn't cutting teeth, so I just got down and stepped forward and dropped my reins over three or four pickets as usual. Just as I turned to go to the gate, one of Mr. Brocker's old dogs discovered us and run up inside the yard and went to barking and raising hell, and Old Bald set back and jerked a whole panel of pickets down. 'Course I was the first thing they hit, and down I went right under his nose, and he did explode and leave there then. I musta rolled twenty foot under them damn pickets before he finally drug 'em over me. He made it another forty or fifty foot before he stopped, and then he just stood there and tromped and kicked till there wasn't nothing left but kindling. I didn't have nothing broke, but I was skinned up like a rodeo mule and didn't have much left of my shirt—and splinters! Them pickets was just rived out with a froe and not drawed down smooth, and I had more dang splinters in me than Doug Berryhill did thorns the time the horse jumped through the plum thicket with him. Time the racket was over, all the Brockers was there and Mrs. Brocker and the girls got me to the house and the old man and the boys got my horse and brought him back. His hind legs was skinned considerable but not so's I couldn't ride him home.

Up till then I'd never been sure just what that girl

thought of me, but whilst the womenfolks had me spread out on the front porch picking out splinters ever'where that was decent, old man Brocker passed and said big a durn fool as I was didn't need nothing but a jackass and a walking stick, and she flew all over him like a banty hen.

Me and her has been married forty years next spring, and I still wonder why she took me when she could have had better men. I guess it's like I heard Mr. Rogers over to Daisetta say once: a woman's love is just like the morning dew, just as apt to fall on a horse biscuit as it is a rose.

Death

WHEN I was about ten, say forty years ago, every child in a small town had some contact with death. Hogs was butchered, chickens killed for Sunday dinner, cattle winter-killed, kittens drowned, unwanted puppies knocked in the head and carried off. All of this was commonplace and we never noticed it very much. Even people dying made very little impression on us unless they was close, like parents or a brother or sister. For most of us it was just grandparents or great-uncles or aunts, and they mostly still lived out in the country and we weren't too well acquainted anyway.

The dead was kept at home and set up with until the funeral, and it mostly meant to us we'd be took out to wherever they was and be expected to act like we was civilized for a day or two. It was usually a most miserable time. We'd be cleaned up and have on our good clothes and even be expected to wear shoes and keep our voices down and not get our clothes dirty nor do anything to shame our parents in front of the kinfolks. This even though there'd be hell's own slew of cousins to run and play and fight with. We'd get out to the barn or away from the house sometimes and try to establish some kind of pecking order, but it never worked out. It couldn't be done without fighting, and that was the one thing we couldn't get by with. Most of us just had the one suit, and who could fight without tearing clothes and getting dirty?

I remember one funeral we went to up in Trinity County, a grandfather, I think, that was the most trying time of my life. I had a girl cousin there, when I think back as pretty a child as I ever saw, that devised a stunt that was the worst on a boy's dignity, which is not the same as adult dignity but just as real, that I ever heard of. Us boys never wore underwear during the day, that was for sleeping in, and some damn fool had invented elastic waistbands for our britches, and this girl cousin would come up behind us, pull our waistband back, and spit right down the crack of our behinds. God, to turn around and see her standing there grinning and know you couldn't hand her a mouth full of knuckles because the ultimate authority, our father, had said no fighting, not for no reason. Even though she loved to travel and raised three children that couldn't ride a car or train a mile without getting carsick, I've never felt like she got her just deserts. I still get flinchy when she's behind me.

One reason the dead never made much of an impression on us was because we never really connected them with who they was. I remember one great-uncle in particular, Uncle Alec Gray, ever' time I saw him he had on old rough clothes, a big dirty hat, and tall boots with mud and cow manure halfway to his knees and was either horseback or working a team. The man they made me look at in the coffin had a suit and tie on, was neat and clean, didn't even have tobacco juice on his chin, and even though I knew it was Uncle Alec, it couldn't be him. I just left it like that and didn't have to face it, I guess was why.

Along maybe a year or two later, I learned what death is. Daisetta was an oil-boom town, started about 1920 after the Hull field come in, and even though most of the workers during my time was in the production end, some of the boomer ways was still around. Whiskey, fighting, and gambling, and women no better than they wanted to be was still pretty much in evidence, and us boys of course knew about all of it. My mother died when my brother and me was four and five, and my Grampa Brett—Grandma Brett had been dead for years—lived with us and helped look after us until Dad went off to the Kilgore oil fields about 1930. Grampa Brett was way up in his seventies and couldn't keep us by hisself, so we went to live with our mother's sister, our Aunt Sudie Penny, and her husband, Uncle Lee. This was supposed to be temporary, but Dad married again, married a woman with five children, and we never lived with him after that, stayed with my mother's kinfolk until we got out on our own.

Now my Aunt Sudie was a fine woman, a hard-working woman who done her best to keep us clean and fed and on the straight and narrow and out of bad company, but I don't think she ever even imagined us like we was. Uncle Lee was a different proposition. He knew boys and we never fooled him a minute, knew better than to try, but he mostly left us alone unless we got too raw and then he just mentioned it and we straightened up.

Living in town, about all the chores we had was sawing and splitting a little heater wood and getting it in the house, and the rest of the time, except for school, we was free. We had to be home at night by seven or eight o'clock, but ever' boy knows the most delicious time is when you're supposed to be but ain't, and we had several ways to get by with staying out. On Saturday we generally worked it like this. We'd get fifteen cents to go to the picture show, always a shoot-'em-up on Saturday, and we'd tell Aunt Sudie instead of going to the matinee we was going over to somebody's house to play and go to the show that night. She knew we'd set through it twice and the second show wouldn't be over until ten thirty, but she'd know where we was and it was all right. We'd go to the matinee—ten cents' admission and a nickel left over for candy, ice cream, or whatever—and after it was over we had until about eleven that night to run the streets and get in and out of whatever mischief we could.

That's the way we'd worked it the night I found out about death. We'd already been all over town, me and Jack and Robert Mansell and two or three more, and was back in front of the picture show when word hit the street that "D" Poe had killed Jack Shaeffer at a bootlegger's place, fighting. We knew where it was, right at the edge of town, we'd slipped around it lots of nights and looked and listened, and we lit out to get in on the excitement. There was five or six people in the backyard, Deputy Sheriff Reid Matthews was there asking questions, and we piled over the board fence and lined up and hoped we wouldn't be noticed and run off.

Well, it was dark as ignorance and we wanted to see something, we didn't care about the questioning and answering, we'd get the straight of it before the law did, anyway (we did, too—every boy in Daisetta knew Jack had been hit with a twenty-four-inch Stilson pipe wrench, but the jury never heard it and they turned Poe loose), so one of the boys, probably Damon Young, he was usually our spokesman, finally got up nerve enough to say, "Where's Jack Shaeffer?"

"Why, right there," Deputy Sheriff Matthews said, and turned his flashlight on the ground right at our feet.

There he was all right, godalmighty, there he was. We was nearly standing on him and he was *dead*. Dead like I'd never seen before. Not neat and clean and well dressed. No, face bruised and bloody, clothes dirty and shirt ripped, eyes wide open and staring, and I knew, knew for the first time, what death was, and it wasn't just laying there quietly and unalive like Uncle Alec. It was the end and forever and final.

I didn't take time to thank Jack for the knowledge. I left when the rest did, about ten seconds after the light hit his face. I did take him home with me, though, and looked at him until I went to sleep and then woke up four or five times and looked at him again. After forty years I can still do it, fresh and clear, when I want to.

Some folks learning about death that young would have made a fine thing out of it toward moral philosophy or religion or some such, but about all it done for me was keep me from fist-fighting in bootleggers' backyards.

A Three-Year-Old Unmarked Boar

THIS yarn is another one told me by Bowen Taylor. Later on I had the same story from R. E. Taylor, but this is Bowen telling it.

"I had a good big bunch of hogs one time stayed close in around that Tin House slough. You know where it is, just above where McMurty had that still, and me and R. E. was down there one time hunting them. Just before we got to the old house, the dogs went to baying up ahead. I had Lindy and my old Rock dog, and R. E. had a little dun dog come from Buddy Caruthers he called Rowdy. Before we could get there, they left running a wild-assed shoat and went out of hearing toward Fishtrap, just a-yow-yow-yow ever' breath.

"I knew Rock and Lindy would quit and come back in a little, so we just pulled up and waited where we was. There was a big old down tree just off from us a little piece, and we was setting there listening for the dogs, and directly I heard a hog pop his teeth out toward it.

" 'Listen, R. E.' I says, 'There's a damn hog right there,' and rode up to where I could see a little better.

"I could see him backed up under some briers and vines between the tree and the first big limb, and I told R. E., 'Come see, it must be one of them old bar's of mine, he sure is a big'un. Looks like he's got four inches of ivory sticking out of his mouth.'

"He rode up and looked and says, 'Come on back before you make him run. When we get the dogs back we'll catch him and carry him out.'

" 'Oh, hell, no,' I told him, 'He ain't going to stay that long, he'll be long gone before them dogs get back.' I studied a little and says, 'R. E., you go down there and come back the other side of that log. I'm going to bay that hog while you catch him.'

" 'You're going to what?' he says. 'You try that and that damn hog is going to rip you down both sides.'

" 'Go on,' I told him, 'We ain't got another chance of getting him.'

"I waited till I seen him come the other side of the clayroot, and got down on my all fours and went to barking and going in towards the old hog, trying to keep him from noticing R. E., and he was popping them teeth and threatening towards me, and directly I pulled back and got my breath and told R. E., 'Hell, come on, R. E., this old dog don't like to fight too close,' and went back to baying, trying not to get so close he'd run at me and still keep him from seeing R. E.

"I was up, I guess, in ten or twelve foot of him, getting hoarser ever' bark and just knowing he'd be on top of me any second, when I seen his behind go up in the air and I says to myself, 'Uh-huh, ol' bully, you waited too long, R. E.'s gottcha.'

"I jumped up and run in and got him by the ears and we laid him down, and I seen I was crazy as R. E. thought I was. It wasn't a bar', it was about a three-year-old unmarked boar.* If I'd knowed that, I'd never pulled that stunt. We had him, though, and I knelt on him while R. E. got a piggin' string out of his leggins pocket and tied him.

---

* In my opinion, and Bowen's also, he was on his hands and knees baying one of the most dangerous animals on either of the American continents.

"After we stood up, R. E. went to laughing and says, 'Bowen, if you had a little better mouth and was a little younger, I believe I could work you awhile with a good dog and make a pretty fair hog dog out of you. You think you could learn to catch?'"

The Education of Robert

ROBERT wanted an education. His mother wanted him to have an education. His pa didn't, and to say his pa was contrary was understating it. People said if he'd took a stand against Noah he'd never admitted to a heavy dew.

Pa was old man Dusay. He'd lived all his life in the Big Thicket and was a market hunter by trade, also by inclination and knack. He farmed ten or twelve acres of corn, enough to feed a horse or two and furnish corn meal for his family. The rest of their living he made selling bear, turkey, and deer—that is, the money part of it. He owned a good many razorback hogs that furnished lard and smoked meat for the table and grease for lye soap. A small bunch of cows furnished his tasso,* milk, and butter. His syrup he traded from his neighbors. Blackberries, mayhaws, and wild grapes could be had for the gathering for his jams, jellies, and a little medicinal wine. His wife raised a good garden every year, had a few chickens, a few geese, and lots of guineas. His only cash outlay was for a few clothes, cloth, powder, shot, sugar, salt, pepper, and a pair of boots or shoes ever' few years. The old man was pretty well fixed and respected —not for his money. Them days a man earned respect by keeping his word and treating his neighbors right, not by the length of his car, the size of his house, and the brand of his suit. He walked with his head up, looked everyone in the eye, and considered himself the equal of any man. Being unable to read the Bible, his religious beliefs were simple.

* Dried meat, like jerky.

He believed there was a God, asked Him for nothing, thanked Him for what he got, and looked up when he prayed.

Mrs. Dusay was entirely different. She was an educated woman who had been a schoolteacher when she'd married the old man. She liked gatherings but was never lonesome by herself. Read the Bible, but had a few private reservations about it. Wished her hens could dodge hawks, fox, and wildcats as well as her guineas could. Was thankful Mr. Dusay was a good provider. Seldom crossed him, but wasn't afraid of him. Went to town twice a year, but didn't need to. Grumbled a little at certain times of the month, but never nagged. Was happy because she felt needed. She pretended to be afraid of thunder when Mr. Dusay was around so he could feel superior. A brother in Houston sent her books on art, philosophy, and religion which she read but never inflicted on other people. She'd saved her egg money for years to help educate her son.

Robert was twelve years old. He'd come along pretty late in his parent's life and had inherited traits from both. He had his mother's self-sufficiency but not her satisfaction at his lot in life. His father's contrariness had come to him as tenacity. Once he decided to do something he went over, under, or through every obstacle. He'd went to a one-room school for four four-month terms and decided he wanted to know more. His mother's brother had offered to keep him and send him to school, and he was determined to go.

A wreck was bound to happen. Mr. Dusay opined that he'd hear no more about school. He intended to teach the boy the market-hunting trade so he'd have a way to make a good living, and intended to start that very night.

He'd noticed where a big old buck deer had been using in back of his field, and figured he'd be worth all of three dollars when toted out of town. It being nigh on to dark, he loaded his gun and split some lighter'd for his fire pan. Along with a good butcher knife, these were the only tools he used, and they bear describing.

His gun was a ten-gauge Remington double that weighed eight and a half pounds. Both barrels were full choke, thirty-two inches long, and made out of twist steel. It had been back to the factory once for new barrels (the first set was shot pretty thin) and a general overhaul. The old man thought the new barrels were just a mite better than the old ones. His fire pan was the shape of a pie plate, but larger and made of iron, and a three-foot-long stick come straight down from the middle of the bottom of it. A fire was built in the pan of fat-lighter'd pine, and it was hoisted over the head and used to shine into the game's eyes. Toting that thing overhead and carrying eight and a half pounds of gun, a man didn't need all night to do a day's work. Having a good population of ground rattlers, copperheads, and cottonmouths in the country, with an occasional timber rattler for variety, the old man and the boy put on their brogan shoes before leaving the house shortly after dark.

The old man knew his trade, because about two hundred yards in the back of the field he looked at that old buck. Easy, easy, he handed the boy back the fire pan, spraddled his legs front and rear for balance, cocked his gun, brought it to his shoulder, and leaned forward so as to take the jolt.

Of course, the boy was excited. He was looking at them eyes as hard as the old man. Looking, peering, getting tenser and tenser, and letting the fire pan tilt further and further forward. With the old man in the position he was, there was a pretty good opening where his brogan had pulled away from the back of his right ankle. The first coal that rolled off the pan centered that opening. Pa's response was instantaneous. He jumped first, high and far, and let out a limb-rattling, leaf-shaking squall, a squall that made panthers for miles around hang their heads in shame. I can't praise that squall too highly. It was just a superlative squall, had everything in it from the moan of a bull gator to the shriek of a blue-darter hawk. It asked for sympathy and demanded attention. A range cow with a baby calf would give that squall the right way.

Mr. Dusay's third action was purely reflexive, but could be termed a mistake, that is, if firing both barrels of a double-barrelled ten-gauge with the stock in the pit of your stomach can be termed a mistake, it was. Mr. Dusay grunted. It was a fine, hearty grunt, not up to the quality of that squall, but nevertheless, one to take note of and remember. Its one fault was, no staying power. It started out about like an old razorback sow when she's startled, and was showing real promise when Mr. Dusay ran out of wind. The rest of his actions was about ordinary and what you'd expect. Just come down flat on his back and laid there, trying to get his breath back. He'd pretty well mashed that coal out en route, but wasn't in any shape to notice, if he hadn't.

While Mr. Dusay was occupied with correcting that mistake he made, let's see what that old buck done. He left. He left and "stayed not in the manner of his going," as the feller said. He had a rack on his head that looked big as a rocking chair, and his first jump hung it in a grapevine ten feet off the ground. This swapped ends with him, and changed his direction, but with that squall in his ears, he cared not. He'd laid in a tree-top once and let two cornbread fed, flagtailed walker dogs boost him out, but that wasn't a patchin' to what he done this time in the dark. Two hours later he was hooking bushes, twenty miles from that squall, and still flinching at every sound. And, now that boy. That buck had nothing on him in the leaving-there department. He left that fire pan with his pa, and nothing preceded him home but that squall. When he got there, it had done moved the chickens and guineas two limbs higher, and made two bar' hogs the old man was fattening tear out of the pen, and had both dogs under the house with every back hair standing up.

Mrs. Dusay was just inside the door, armed with a kettle of boiling water. This was a fearsome weapon in the hands of a determined woman. She'd about decided that no one but Gabriel could make a sound like that, and was mentally revising some of her reservations about the Book when the boy went to hollering "Mama!" and come through the door and slid under the bed. She'd got him out and had him pretty well gentled down when she heard the old man come across the porch. She looked up to see him standing in the door, a shoe in one hand and a sack in the other. He'd come by the barn, got a good stiff drink out of a jug he had cached there, and dug up a rawhide sack from the corner of a horse stall. This was his bank and contained his life savings. Being a realist, he had it all in gold.

The boy went to dodging and fighting his head when he seen his pa, but Mrs. Dusay got him soothed and standing quiet by the time the old man crossed the room.

"Woman," he said as he dropped the bag on the bed, "woman, I'm an old man, and I don't believe I can stand the wear and tear of teaching that boy a trade. Send him to school, and may the Lord preserve his teachers."

That boy went to school, got interested in theology, and come out a minister, and people looking for a way to heaven without dying aggravated the hell out of him the rest of his life.

www.ingramcontent.com/pod-product-compliance
Lightning Source LLC
Chambersburg PA
CBHW030330080526
44584CB00012B/803